1001
SMARTEST
THINGS
EVER SAID

1001
SMARTEST
THINGS
EVER SAID

Edited and with an Introduction by

Steven D. Price

THE LYONS PRESS
Guilford, Connecticut
An imprint of The Globe Pequot Press

The Lyons Press is an imprint of The Globe Pequot Press.

10 9 8 7 6 5 4 3 2

Printed in the United States of America

Designed by Carol Sawyer/Rose Design

ISBN 1-59228-266-0

Library of Congress Cataloging-in-Publication Data is available on file.

CONTENTS

I quote others only in order the better to express myself.

—*Michel de Montaigne*

INTRODUCTION

What qualifies an utterance to be among the smartest things ever said? In other words, what do we mean by "smart?"

Mental alertness or resourcefulness is one meaning, and you'll find that all the entries in this compendium share that quality: a perceptiveness with regard to the human condition in its many manifestations.

"Smart" also means stylish ("that dress looks smart on you"), and many of the entries are indeed elegant in their use of language. Witty too, both in their cleverness and in the eighteenth-century use of the word that meant "good sense": Alexander Pope said it best when he wrote that "true wit is Nature to advantage dressed / What oft was said but ne'er so well expressed."

Smart also means a sharp pain ("ouch, that smarts!"). Many of the entries provoke just such a response: a shock of recognition or an uncomfortable jolt to our prejudices and preconceptions.

One category, however, will not seem full of paradigms of originality, and that is proverbs. The very nature of proverbs involves a lack of originality; they epitomize "what oft was said." But to find them unoriginal or, worse, time-worn clichés, is to miss the point. Proverbs are time-worn because they have been used so much; if they did not contain so much distilled folk wisdom that speaks to new generations with renewed vigor, they would have disappeared through the very same folk process by which they were created.

The range of these quotations—as many written as having been spoken—touches every human situation and activity. Those in "Life and Death (And Some of What Happens in Between)" span from the cradle to the grave. "The Life of the Mind" examines the intellectual, while interpersonal relationships are the subject of "Love and Friendship." Both the spiritual and the worldly figure prominently in "Success, and Ways to Achieve It" and "Politics and Politicians, Government and Statesmen." "Proverbs" is a concentration of just that, although many other proverbs appear where and when especially relevant in other chapters.

The contributors consist of no less a wide range. William Shakespeare and Yogi Berra, the Bible and Joseph Stalin, Dwight Eisenhower and Keith Richards and Mick Jagger—strange bedfellows perhaps, but that simply demonstrates that there is no monopoly on wisdom.

The criteria by which a quotation qualified for inclusion among the 1001 *Smartest* boiled down to profundity and variety. Although some readers may take issue with what has been included and, equally intriguing, what has been omitted, that is their—that is to say, your—right and privilege. And lest someone point out that some entries contradict others, as in "absence makes the heart grow fonder" or "out of sight, out of mind," the very nature of human wisdom is often contractory.

Which entry in the entire book qualifies as the smartest? Although wisdom is seldom a competition sport, that's a question I've been asked, and more than once. My response is to share the memory of a television drama from the 1950s, on a series that older readers may recall as *Four Star Playhouse.* The setting was a bar into which a group of people had wandered to seek companionship in face of the world's coming to an end (I can't recall how or why, but Armageddon was nigh). One of the patrons had a computer—very much a novelty fifty years ago—into which he had entered all of the world's literature. Surrounded by the other patrons, he then asked the computer to answer the question, "how can the world be saved?"

After much whirring of gears and flashing of lights (remember, this was the '50s), the answer began: "I am the Lord Thy God; Thou shalt have no other god before me. . . ." and thereafter followed the rest of the Ten Commandments. One writer's opinion, but certainly food for thought.

Much has changed in the past fifty years. True wisdom, however, has not because it does not; truth abideth forever. In a society that has been accused of taking dumbing-down to new heights (or depths), studying the wisdom of the ages is a vital step in regaining intellectual and ethical standards.

STEVEN D. PRICE
NEW YORK, N.Y.
MAY, 2004

I.

LIFE
AND
DEATH

(And Some of What Happens in Between)

Life can only be understood backwards; but it must be lived forwards.

—*Søren Kierkegaard*

There is no cure for birth and death save to enjoy the interval.

—*George Santayana*

The future you shall know when it has come; before then forget it.

—*Aeschylus*

One's own thought is one's world. What a person thinks is what he becomes.

—*Maitri Upanishads*

Time ripens all things; no man is born wise.

—*Miguel de Cervantes*

A baby is God's opinion that life should go on.

—*Carl Sandburg*

It is easier for a father to have children than for children to have a real father.

—*Pope John XXIII*

The most important question in the world is, "Why is the child crying?"

—*Alice Walker*

If you can give your son or daughter only one gift, let it be enthusiasm.

—*Bruce Barton*

If there is anything we wish to change in the child, we should first examine it and see whether it is not something that could better be changed in ourselves.

—*Carl Jung*

Ain't no man can avoid being born average, but there ain't no man got to be common.

—*Satchel Paige*

I am afraid we must make the world honest before we can honestly say to our children that honesty is the best policy.

—*Sir Walter Besant*

You can learn many things from children. How much patience you have, for instance.

—*Franklin P. Adams*

Acting childish seems to come naturally, but acting like an adult, no matter how old we are, just doesn't come easy to us.

—*Lily Tomlin*

My father always said there are four things a child needs: plenty of love, nourishing food, regular sleep, and lots of soap and water. After that, what he needs most is some intelligent neglect.

—*Ivy Baker Priest*

A birthday is a good time to begin anew: throwing away the old habits, as you would old clothes, and never putting them on again.

—*Bronson Alcott*

Growth is the only evidence of life.

—*John Henry Newman*

The hardest thing to learn in life is which bridge to cross and which to burn.

—*David Russell*

Some people are so much sunshine to the square inch.

—*Walt Whitman*

The most difficult thing in the world is to know how to do a thing and to watch someone else do it wrong, without comment.

—*T. H. White*

"If everybody minded their own business," the Duchess said in a hoarse growl, "the world would go round a good deal faster than it does."

—*Lewis Carroll*

Live a life as a monument to your soul.

—*Ayn Rand*

If you're in a card game and you don't know who the sucker is, you're it.

—*Anonymous*

Too many people are thinking of security instead of opportunity. They seem more afraid of life than death.

—*James F. Byrnes*

We boil at different degrees.

—*Ralph Waldo Emerson*

I would feel more optimistic about a bright future for man if he spent less time proving that he can outwit Nature and more time tasting her sweetness and respecting her seniority.

—*E. B. White*

No man is a hero to his own valet.

—*Anonymous*

Men occassionally stumble over the truth, but most of them pick themselves up and hurry on as if nothing had happened.

—Sir Winston Churchill

Service to others is the rent you pay for your room here on earth.

—Muhammad Ali

The best and safest thing is to keep a balance in your life, acknowledge the great powers around us and in us. If you can do that, and live that way, you are really a wise man.

—Euripides

Life is a great big canvas; throw all the paint you can at it.

—*Danny Kaye*

You gain strength, courage and confidence by every experience in which you really stop to look fear in the face. You are able to say to yourself, "I lived through this horror. I can take the next thing that comes along."

—*Eleanor Roosevelt*

The point of music is discovered in every moment of playing and listening to it. It is the same, I feel, with the greater part of our lives, and if we are unduly absorbed in improving them we may forget altogether to live them.

—*Alan B. Watts*

Nearly all men can stand adversity, but if you want to test a man's character, give him power.

—*Abraham Lincoln*

On the whole, human beings want to be good, but not too good and not quite all the time.

—*George Orwell*

This above all: to thine own self be true,
And it must follow, as the night the day,
Thou canst not then be false to any man.

—*William Shakespeare*

Know how sublime a thing is to suffer and be strong.

—*Henry Wadsworth Longfellow*

Be more concerned with your character than your reputation, because your character is what you really are, while your reputation is merely what others think you are.

—*John R. Wooden*

Education is the best provision for the journey to old age.

—*Aristotle*

I am never afraid of what I know.

—Anna Sewell

Never be haughty to the humble; never be humble to the haughty.

—Jefferson Davis

It is extraordinary how extraordinary the ordinary person is.

—George F. Will

The majority of men are bundles of beginnings.
—*Ralph Waldo Emerson*

Contemplate thy powers, contemplate thy wants and thy connections; so shalt thou discover the duties of life, and be directed in all thy ways.
—*Akhenaton*

The childhood shows the man, as morning shows the day.
—*John Milton*

The young always have the same problem—how to rebel and conform at the same time. They have solved this by defying their parents and copying one another.

—*Quentin Crisp*

Who does not grow, declines.

—*Rabbi Hillel*

There is no reason why the same man should like the same book at 18 and at 48.

—*Ezra Pound*

The man who views the world at 50 the same as he did at 20 has wasted thirty years of his life.

—*Muhammad Ali*

If all misfortunes were laid in one common heap whence everyone must take an equal portion, most people would be contented to take their own and depart.

—*Socrates*

Many people genuinely do not wish to be saints, and it is possible that some who achieve or aspire to sainthood have never had much temptation to be human beings.

—*George Orwell*

Don't judge each day by the harvest you reap, but by the seeds you plant.
—*Robert Louis Stevenson*

If you can spend a perfectly useless afternoon in a perfectly useless manner, you have learned how to live.
—*Lin Yutang*

The man who insists upon seeing with perfect clearness before he decides, never decides. Accept life, and you must accept regret.
—*Henri Frédéric Amiel*

He has great tranquility of heart who cares neither for the praises nor the fault-finding of men.

—*Honoré de Balzac*

One reason why birds and horses are not unhappy is because they are not trying to impress other birds and horses.

—*Dale Carnegie*

To say yes, you have to sweat and roll up your sleeves and plunge both hands into life up to the elbows. It's easy to say no, even if it means dying.

—*Jean Anouilh*

A dead thing can go with the stream, but only a living thing can go against it.

—G. K. Chesterton

When you are younger you get blamed for crimes you never committed and when you're older you begin to get credit for virtues you never possessed. It evens itself out.

—George Santayana

Life is an echo. What you send out—you get back. What you give— you get.

—Anonymous

Life is like playing a violin in public and learning the instrument as one goes on.

—*Samuel Butler*

Life consists not in holding good cards but in playing those you hold well.

—*Josh Billings*

Life is an adventure in forgiveness.

—*Norman Cousins*

Life is the art of drawing sufficient conclusions from insufficient premises.

—*Samuel Butler*

If you can't make it better, you can laugh at it.

—*Erma Bombeck*

Character is much easier kept than recovered.

—*Thomas Paine*

This is the first test of a gentleman: his respect for those who can be of no possible value to him.

—*William Lyon Phelps*

The future comes one day at a time.

—*Dean Acheson*

Do well and you will have no need for ancestors.

—*Voltaire*

The strongest man in the world is he who stands alone.

—Henrik Ibsen

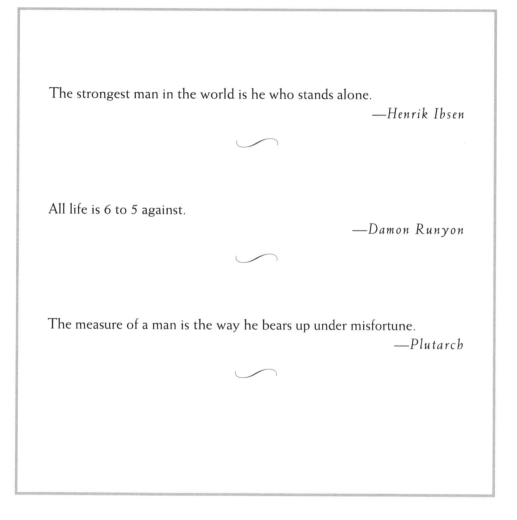

All life is 6 to 5 against.

—Damon Runyon

The measure of a man is the way he bears up under misfortune.

—Plutarch

Hope springs eternal in the human breast: / Man never is, but always to be blest.

—Alexander Pope

A mature person is one who does not think only in absolutes, who is able to be objective even when deeply stirred emotionally, who has learned that there is both good and bad in all people and all things, and who walks humbly and deals charitably with the circumstances of life.

—Eleanor Roosevelt

The moment we begin to fear the opinions of others and hesitate to tell the truth that is in us, and from motives of policy are silent when we should speak, the divine floods of light and life no longer flow into our souls.

—Elizabeth Cady Stanton

It is not only for what we do that we are held responsible, but also for what we do not do.

—Molière

People travel to wonder at the height of the mountains, at the huge waves of the seas, at the long course of the rivers, at the vast compass of the ocean, at the circular motion of the stars, and yet they pass by themselves without wondering.

—Saint Augustine

Time is the wisest counselor.

—Pericles

Happy the man, and happy he alone,
He who can call today his own:
He who, secure within, can say,
Tomorrow do thy worst, for I have lived today.
Be fair or foul or rain or shine
The joys I have possessed, in spite of fate, are mine.
Not Heaven itself upon the past has power,
But what has been, has been, and I have had my hour.

—*Horace*

The older I grow the more I distrust the familiar doctrine that age brings wisdom.

—*H. L. Mencken*

Go confidently in the direction of your dreams! Live the life you've imagined. As you simplify your life, the laws of the universe will be simpler.

—*Henry David Thoreau*

I do not believe that sheer suffering teaches. If suffering alone taught, all the world would be wise, since everyone suffers. To suffering must be added mourning, understanding, patience, love, openness and the willingness to remain vulnerable.

—Joseph Addison

. . . before I can live with other folks I've got to live with myself. The one thing that doesn't abide by majority rule is a person's conscience.

—Harper Lee

Never feel self-pity, the most destructive emotion there is. How awful to be caught up in the terrible squirrel cage of self.

—Millicent Fenwick

A halo has to fall only a few inches to be a noose.

—*Anonymous*

If you cry because the sun has gone out of your life, your tears will prevent you from seeing the stars.

—*Rabindranath Tagore*

A man's heart away from nature becomes hard; lack of respect for growing, living things soon leads to a lack of respect for humans too.

—*Luther Standing Bear*

Happiness is always a by-product. It is probably a matter of temperament, and for anything I know it may be glandular. But it is not something that can be demanded from life, and if you are not happy you had better stop worrying about it.

—*Robertson Davies*

Live your questions now, and perhaps even without knowing it, you will live along some distant day into your answers.

—*Rainer Maria Rilke*

Be grateful for luck. Pay the thunder no mind—listen to the birds. And don't hate nobody.

—*Eubie Blake*

May you have a strong foundation when the winds of changes shift . . . and may you be forever young.

—*Bob Dylan*

Do not go where the path may lead, go instead where there is no path and leave a trail.

—*Ralph Waldo Emerson*

Growth demands a temporary surrender of security.

—*Gail Sheehy*

The mass of men lead lives of quiet desperation.

—Henry David Thoreau

Reflect upon your present blessings, of which every man has plenty; not on your past misfortunes of which all men have some.

—Charles Dickens

Never let yesterday use up too much of today.

—Will Rogers

I can resist everything except temptation.

—*Oscar Wilde*

To succeed in life, you need two things: ignorance and confidence.

—*Mark Twain*

Expect nothing. Live frugally on surprise.

—*Alice Walker*

A man cannot be too careful in his choice of enemies.

—*Oscar Wilde*

A great secret of success is to go through life as a man who never gets used up.

—*Albert Schweitzer*

Just trust yourself, then you will know how to live.

—*Johann Wolfgang von Goethe*

A man of good will with a little effort and belief in his own powers can enjoy a deep, tranquil, rich life—provided he go his own way. . . . To live one's own life is still the best way of life, always was, and always will be.

—Henry Miller

If only I may grow: firmer, simpler—quieter, warmer.

—Dag Hammarskjöld

You can outdistance that which is running after you, but not what is running inside you.

—Rwandan proverb

This existence of ours is as transient as autumn clouds. To watch the birth and death of beings is like looking at the movements of a dance. A lifetime is a flash of lightning in the sky. Rushing by, like a torrent down a steep mountain.

—Buddha

We are here to laugh at the odds and live our lives so well that Death will tremble to take us.

—Charles Bukowski

Death is nothing to us, since when we are, death has not come, and when death has come, we are not.

—Epicurus

We are no more than candles burning in the wind.

—*Japanese proverb*

Live so that you wouldn't be ashamed to sell the family parrot to the town gossip.

—*Will Rogers*

All would live long, but none would be old.

—*Benjamin Franklin*

It is in self-limitation that a master first shows himself.

—*Johann Wolfgang von Goethe*

In the long run, we shape our lives, and we shape ourselves. The process never ends until we die. And the choices we make are ultimately our own responsibility.

—*Eleanor Roosevelt*

The mere process of growing old together will make the slightest acquaintance seem a bosom friend.

—*Logan Pearsall Smith*

You are never too old to be what you might have been.

—*George Eliot*

If I knew I was going to live this long, I'd have taken better care of myself.

—*Mickey Mantle*

I went to the woods because I wished to live deliberately, to front only the essential facts of life and see if I could not learn what they had to teach; and not, when I came to die, discover that I had not lived.

—*Henry David Thoreau, "Walden"*

People—some good, some bad, but in the long run we come out even.

—*Jan Hittle*

The trouble with quotes about death is that 99.999 percent of them are made by people who are still alive.

—*Joshua Bruns*

As a well-spent day brings happy sleep, so a life well spent brings happy death.

—*Leonardo da Vinci*

In an artist's life, death is perhaps not the most difficult thing.

—*Vincent van Gogh*

Death—the last sleep? No, it is the final awakening.

—*Sir Walter Scott*

Lord, how the day passes! It's like a life—so quickly when we don't watch it and so slowly if we do.

—*John Steinbeck*

I have discovered that all human evil comes from this: man's being unable to sit still and quiet in a room alone.

—*Blaise Pascal*

It is said an Eastern monarch once charged his wise men to invent him a sentence, to be ever in view, and which should be true and appropriate in all times and situations. They presented him the words: And this, too, shall pass away.

—*Abraham Lincoln*

No man is an Island, entire of itself; every man is a piece of the Continent, a part of the main; if a clod be washed away by the sea, Europe is the less, as well as if a promontory were, as well as if a manor of thy friends or of thine own were; any man's death diminishes me, because I am involved in Mankind; And therefore never send to know for whom the bell tolls; It tolls for thee.

—*John Donne*

I want to live my life so that my nights are not full of regrets.

—*D. H. Lawrence*

I promise to keep on living as though I expected to live forever. Nobody grows old by merely living a number of years. People grow old by deserting their ideals. Years may wrinkle the skin, but to give up wrinkles the soul.

—*Douglas MacArthur*

May you live all the days of your life.

—*Jonathan Swift*

Live simply, that others may simply live.

—Mohandas Gandhi

Keep on truckin'.

—Robert Crumb

Hope is a good breakfast, but it is a bad supper.

—Sir Francis Bacon

My advice to you is not to inquire why or whither, but just enjoy your ice cream while it's on your plate—that's my philosophy.

—*Thornton Wilder*

Enjoy the spring of love and youth,
To some good angel leave the rest;
For time will teach thee soon the truth,
There are no birds in last year's nest.

—*Henry Wadsworth Longfellow*

Know the true value of time; snatch, seize, and enjoy every moment of it. No idleness, no laziness, no procrastination: never put off till to-morrow what you can do to-day.

—*Philip Dormer Stanhope, Lord Chesterfield*

Let us not look back in anger, nor forward in fear, but around in awareness.

—*James Thurber*

Experience is a hard teacher. She gives the test first and the lessons afterwards.

—*Anonymous*

No man is rich enough to buy back his past.

—*Oscar Wilde*

In times like these, it helps to recall that there have always been times like these.

—*Paul Harvey*

Make voyages! Attempt them . . . there's nothing else.

—*Tennessee Williams*

The best portion of a good man's life is his little, nameless, unremembered acts of kindness and of love.

—*William Wordsworth*

The years between fifty and seventy are the hardest. You are always being asked to do things, and yet you are not decrepit enough to turn them down.

—T. S. Eliot

Men are like wine, some turn to vinegar, but the best improve with age.

—Pope John XXIII

Grow old along with me! / The best is yet to be.

—Robert Browning

The only man who behaves sensibly is my tailor; he takes my measure anew every time he sees me, whilst all the rest go on with their old measurements, and expect them to fit me.

—George Bernard Shaw

One of the secrets of a long and fruitful life is to forgive everybody everything every night before you go to bed.

—Bernard Mannes Baruch

Old age ain't no place for sissies.

—Bette Davis

Don't look back. Something might be gaining on you.

—*Satchel Paige*

Don't hurry, don't worry. You're here for a short visit. So be sure to stop and smell the flowers.

—*Walter Hagen*

Live as long as you can. Die when you can't help it.

—*James Brown*

A person will be called to account on Judgment Day for every permissible thing he might have enjoyed but did not.

—*The Talmud*

Millions long for immortality who do not know what to do with themselves on a rainy Sunday afternoon.

—*Susan Ertz*

Old age is like everything else. To make a success of it, you've got to start young.

—*Fred Astaire*

Since time is not a person we can overtake when he is past, let us honor him with mirth and cheerfulness of heart while he is passing.

—*Johann Wolfgang von Goethe*

I shall tell you a great secret my friend. Do not wait for the last judgement, it takes place every day.

—*Albert Camus*

To be idle is a short road to death and to be diligent is a way of life; foolish people are idle, wise people are diligent.

—*Buddha*

I have in irrepressible desire to live till I can be assured that the world is a little better for my having lived in it.

—*Abraham Lincoln*

Man is the only animal that blushes. Or needs to.

—*Mark Twain*

The tragedy of life is not so much what men suffer, but rather what they miss.

—*Thomas Carlyle*

The greatest thing in life is to die young—but delay it as long as possible.

—George Bernard Shaw

I like living. I have sometimes been wildly, despairingly, acutely miserable, racked with sorrow, but through it all I still know quite certainly that just to be alive is a grand thing.

—Agatha Christie

Taking joy in life is a woman's best cosmetic.

—Rosalind Russell

The greatest pleasure in life is doing what people say you cannot do.

—*Walter Bagehot*

The difference between life and the movies is that a script has to make sense, and life doesn't.

—*Joseph L. Mankiewicz*

Never, never rest contented with any circle of ideas, but always be certain that a wider one is still possible.

—*Pearl Bailey*

It is hard to have patience with people who say There is no death or Death doesn't matter. There is death. And whatever is matters. And whatever happens has consequences, and it and they are irrevocable and irreversible. You might as well say that birth doesn't matter.

—*C. S. Lewis*

Judge a man by his questions rather than his answers.

—*Voltaire*

Things are seldom what they seem.

—*Sir William S. Gilbert*

Good advice is something a man gives when he is too old to set a bad example.

—*François de La Rochefoucauld*

The bitterest tears shed over graves are for words left unsaid and deeds left undone.

—*Harriet Beecher Stowe*

God not only plays dice, he throws them in the corner where you can't see them.

—*Stephen Hawking*

There is, therefore, only one categorical imperative. It is: Act only according to that maxim by which you can at the same time will that it should become a universal law.

—Immanuel Kant

How wonderful it is that nobody need wait a single moment before starting to improve the world.

—Anne Frank

What the superior man seeks is in himself. What the mean man seeks is in others.

—Confucius

Courage is contagious. When a brave man takes a stand, the spines of others are stiffened.

—*Billy Graham*

Lying to ourselves is more deeply ingrained than lying to others.

—*Fyodor Mikhaylovich Dostoyevsky*

Cowards die many times before their deaths; The valiant never taste death but once.

—*William Shakespeare*

Hateful to me as the gates of Hades is that man who hides one thing in his heart and speaks another.

—*Homer*

Your vision will become clear only when you can look into your own heart. Who looks outside, dreams; who looks inside, awakens.

—*Carl Jung*

It is a human nature to think wisely and act foolishly.

—*Antatole France*

Everything should be as simple as it is, but not simpler.

—Albert Einstein

A man has to live with himself, and he should see to it that he always has good company.

—Charles Evans Hughes

Wealth and children are the adornment of this present life, but good works, which are lasting, are better in the sight of thy Lord as to recompense, and better as to hope.

—The Koran

If you enjoy living, it is not difficult to keep the sense of wonder.

—*Ray Bradbury*

Words make you think a thought. Music makes you feel a feeling. A song makes you feel a thought.

—*E.Y. Harburg*

Worry is like a rocking chair, it will give you something to do, but it won't get you anywhere.

—*Anonymous*

Silence is argument carried on by other means.

—*Ernesto "Che" Guevara*

To do just the opposite is also a form of imitation.

—*Georg Christoph Lichtenberg*

The gentle mind by gentle deeds is known. For a man by nothing is so well betrayed, as by his manners.

—*Edmund Spenser*

He who angers you conquers you.

—*Elizabeth Kenny*

Believe not because some old manuscripts are produced, believe not because it is your national belief, believe not because you have been made to believe from your childhood, but reason truth out, and after you have analyzed it, then if you find it will do good to one and all, believe it, live up to it and help others live up to it.

—*Buddha*

The line dividing good and evil cuts through the heart of every human being. And who is willing to destroy a piece of his own heart?

—*Aleksandr Solzhenitsyn*

He who forgiveth, and is reconciled unto his enemy, shall receive his reward from God; for he loveth not the unjust doers.

—*The Koran*

Let us then suppose the mind to be, as we say, a white paper, void of all characters, without any ideas. How comes it to be furnished? . . . To this I answer, in one word, from experience.

—*John Locke*

He that troubleth his own house shall inherit the wind.

—*The Bible, Proverbs 11:29*

Everyone can master a grief but he that has it.

—*William Shakespeare*

As through this world I rambled
I've seen lots of funny men.
Some will rob you with a six-gun
And some with a fountain pen.

—*Woody Guthrie*

As blushing will sometimes make a whore pass for a virtuous woman, so modesty may make a fool seem a man of sense.

—*Jonathan Swift*

Without music, life is a journey through a desert.

—*Pat Conroy*

Sooner or later we all discover that the important moments in life are not the advertised ones, not the birthdays, the graduations, the weddings, not the great goals achieved. The real milestones are less prepossessing. They come to the door of memory unannounced, stray dogs that amble in, sniff around a bit and simply never leave. Our lives are measured by these.

—*Susan B. Anthony*

Use your health, even to the point of wearing it out. That is what it is for. Spend all you have before you die; and do not outlive yourself.

—*George Bernard Shaw*

Whoever destroys a single life is as guilty as though he had destroyed the entire world; and whoever rescues a single life earns as much merit as though he had rescued the entire world.

—*The Talmud*

Age is a question of mind over matter. If you don't mind, it doesn't matter.

—*Satchel Paige*

For of all sad words of tongue or pen / the saddest are these; It might have been!

—*John Greenleaf Whittier*

A thing is not necessarily true because a man dies for it.

—*Oscar Wilde*

Wrinkles should merely indicate where smiles have been.

—*Mark Twain*

Growing old is no more than a bad habit that a busy person has not time to form.

—*André Maurois*

If you think about disaster, you will get it. Brood about death and you hasten your demise. Think positively and masterfully, with confidence and faith, and life becomes more secure, more fraught with action, richer in achievement and experience.

—*Swami Sivananda*

The act of dying is also one of the acts of life.

—*Marcus Aurelius*

The Moving Finger writes; and having writ,
Moves on; nor all your Piety nor Wit
Shall lure it back to cancel half a Line,
Nor all your Tears wash out a Word of it.

—*Omar Khayyam*

Old age is far more than white hair, wrinkles, the feeling that it is too late and the game finished, that the stage belongs to the rising generations. The true evil is not the weakening of the body, but the indifference of the soul.

—*André Maurois*

When you're young and you fall off a horse, you may break something. When you're my age and you fall off, you splatter.

—*Roy Rogers*

When the great scorer comes to write against your name, he marks not that you won or lost, but how you played the game.

—*Grantland Rice*

A lifetime of happiness! No man alive could bear it: it would be hell on earth.

—*George Bernard Shaw*

Old minds are like old horses; you must exercise them if you wish to keep them in working order.

—*John Adams*

I wasted time, and now doth time waste me.

—*William Shakespeare*

Anyone who keeps the ability to see beauty in every age of life really never grows old.

—*Franz Kafka*

Life is like a game of cards. The hand you are dealt is determinism; the way you play it is free will.

—*Jawaharlal Nehru*

We can easily forgive a child who is afraid of the dark. The real tragedy of life is when men are afraid of the light.

—*Plato*

And we should consider every day lost on which we have not danced at least once. And we should call every truth false which was not accompanied by at least one laugh.

—*Friedrich Wilhelm Nietzsche*

We don't see things as they are, we see them as we are.

—*Anaïs Nin*

The happy man is not he who seems thus to others, but who seems thus to himself.

—*Marcel Proust*

When you betray somebody else, you also betray yourself.
—*Isaac Bashevis Singer*

No matter how dark things seem to be or actually are, raise your sights and see the possibilities—always see them, for they're always there.
—*Norman Vincent Peale*

In order for three people to keep a secret, two must be dead.
—*Benjamin Franklin*

In the majority of sane human lives there is no problem of sex at all; there is no problem of marriage at all; there is no problem of tempera-ment at all; for all these problems are dwarfed and rendered ridiculous by the standing problem of being a moderately honest man and paying the butcher.

—*G. K. Chesterton*

Three o'clock is always too late or too early for anything you want to do.

—*Jean-Paul Sartre*

My hopes are not always realized, but I always hope.

—*Ovid*

Sometimes a cigar is just a cigar.

—Sigmund Freud

All is for the best in the best of all possible worlds.

—Voltaire

Whatever befalls the earth befalls the sons and daughters of the earth. We did not weave the web of life; We are merely a strand in it. What we do with the web, we do to ourselves . . .

—Chief Seattle

The world is full of magical things patiently waiting for our wits to grow sharper.

—Bertrand Russell

The best remedy for anger is delay.

—Brigham Young

Live well. It is the greatest revenge.

—The Talmud

A ship ought not to be held by one anchor, nor life by a single hope.

—*Epictetus*

I keep my ideals, because in spite of everything I still believe that people are really good at heart.

—*Anne Frank*

A community is like a ship, everyone ought to be prepared to take the helm.

—*Henrik Ibsen*

Sometimes our light goes out but is blown into flame by another human being. Each of us owes deepest thanks to those who have rekindled this light.

—Albert Schweitzer

Life does not cease to be funny when people die any more than it ceases to be serious when people laugh.

—Antoine de Saint-Exupéry

Desire is half of life, indifference is half of death.

—Kahlil Gibran

Life is pleasant. Death is peaceful. It's the transition that's troublesome.

—*Isaac Asimov*

The great consolation in life is to say what one thinks.

—*Voltaire*

Men fear death, as children fear to go in the dark; and as that natural fear in children is increased with tales, so is the other.

—*Sir Francis Bacon*

If man hasn't discovered something that he will die for, he isn't fit to live.
—Martin Luther King, Jr.

Death is not extinguishing the light; it is putting out the lamp because dawn has come.

—Rabindranath Tagore

Be of good cheer about death and know this as a truth—that no evil can happen to a good man, either in life or after death.

—Socrates

I said to Life, "I would hear Death speak." And Life raised her voice a little higher and said, "You hear him now."

—*Kahlil Gibran*

The riders in a race do not stop short when they reach the goal. There is a little finishing canter before they come to a standstill. . . . The canter that brings you to a standstill need not be only coming to rest. It cannot be while you still live.

—*Oliver Wendell Holmes, Jr.*

Our fear of death is like our fear that summer will be short, but when we have had our swing of pleasure, our fill of fruit, and our swelter of heat, we say we have had our day.

—*Ralph Waldo Emerson*

Sweet is a grief well ended.

—Aeschylus

To be able to look back upon one's life in satisfaction, is to live twice.
—Kahlil Gibran

The longer I live, the more beautiful life becomes.
—Frank Lloyd Wright

It's not over until it's over.

—*Yogi Berra*

When I look back on all these worries, I remember the story of the old man who said on his deathbed that he had had a lot of trouble in his life, most of which had never happened.

—*Sir Winston Churchill*

Neither fire nor wind, birth nor death can erase our good deeds.

—*Buddha*

Death ends a life, not a relationship.

—*Jack Lemmon*

I decline to accept the end of man. It is easy enough to say that man is immortal because he will endure: that when the last ding-dong of doom has clanged and faded from the last worthless rock hanging tideless in the last red and dying evening, that even then there will still be one more sound: that of his puny inexhaustible voice, still talking. I refuse to accept this. I believe that man will not merely endure: he will prevail. He is immortal, not because he alone among creatures has an inexhaustible voice, but because he has a soul, a spirit capable of compassion and sacrifice and endurance.

—William Faulkner

Fear not for the future, weep not for the past.

—Percy Bysshe Shelley

I speak truth, not so much as I would, but as much as I dare; and I dare a little more, as I grow older.

—Catherine Drinker Bowen

How far you go in life depends on your being tender with the young, compassionate with the aged, sympathetic with the striving, and tolerant of the weak and strong. Because someday in your life you will have been all of these.

—*George Washington Carver*

I always remember an epitaph which is in the cemetery at Tombstone, Arizona. It says: "Here lies Jack Williams. He done his damnedest."
I think that is the greatest epitaph a man can have.

—*Harry S. Truman*

In the end, everything is a gag.

—*Charlie Chaplin*

II

LOVE
AND
FRIENDSHIP

What is a friend? A single soul dwelling in two bodies.

—*Aristotle*

Always be a little kinder than necessary.

—*Sir James Matthew Barrie*

People are unreasonable, illogical, and self-centered. Love them anyway.

—*Mother Teresa*

To err is human, to forgive divine.

—*Alexander Pope*

To err is human; to forgive, infrequent.

—*Franklin P. Adams*

A person is only as good as what they love.

—*Saul Bellow*

And in the end, the love you take is equal to the love you make.

—*Paul McCartney*

To give counsel as well as to take it is a feature of true friendship.

—*Marcus Tullius Cicero*

Thousands of candles can be lighted from a single candle, And the life of the candle will not be shortened. Happiness never decreases by being shared.

—*Buddha*

Kind hearts are more than coronets / And simple faith than Norman blood.

—Alfred, Lord Tennyson

Laughter is the closest distance between two people.

—Victor Borge

A heart can be broken, but it will keep beating just the same.

—Fanny Flagg

Love is like war; easy to begin but very hard to stop.

—*H. L. Mencken*

It is well, when judging a friend, to remember that he is judging you with the same godlike and superior impartiality.

—*Arnold Bennett*

Though you break your heart, men will go on as before.

—*Marcus Aurelius*

I count myself in nothing else so happy / As in a soul rememb'ring my good friends.

—*William Shakespeare*

The heart has its reasons of which reason knows nothing.

—*Blaise Pascal*

Have a heart that never hardens, a temper that never tires, a touch that never hurts.

—*Charles Dickens*

Few men have the natural strength to honour a friend's success without envy.

—*Aeschylus*

There might be some credit in being jolly.

—*Charles Dickens*

Kind words do not cost much. They never blister the tongue or lips. They make other people good-natured. They also produce their own image on men's souls, and a beautiful image it is.

—*Blaise Pascal*

To give pleasure to a single heart by a single kind act is better than a thousand head-bowings in prayer.

—Saadi

Goodness does not consist in greatness, but greatness in goodness.

—Athenaeus

How should we like it / were stars to burn / With a passion for us we / could not return / If equal affection there cannot be / Let the more loving one be me.

—W. H. Auden

Love is a great beautifier.

—Louisa May Alcott

If you have only one smile in you, give it to the people you love. Don't be surly at home, then go out in the street and start grinning "Good morning" at total strangers.

—Maya Angelou

Without friends no one would choose to live, though he had all other goods.

—Aristotle

An insincere and evil friend is more to be feared than a wild beast; a wild beast may wound your body, but an evil friend will wound your mind.

—*Buddha*

It is a good thing to be rich and a good thing to be strong, but it is a better thing to be loved by many friends.

—*Euripides*

It's sad when someone you know becomes someone you knew.

—*Henry Rollins*

Your friends will know you better in the first moment you meet than your acquaintances will know you in a lifetime.

—*Richard Bach*

It is in pardoning that we are pardoned.

—*Saint Francis of Assisi*

In those whom I like, I can find no common denominator; in those whom I love I can: they all make me laugh.

—*W. H. Auden*

Those who bring sunshine to the lives of others cannot keep it from themselves.

—*Sir James Matthew Barrie*

The person who tries to live alone will not succeed as a human being. His heart withers if it does not answer another heart. His mind shrinks away if he hears only the echoes of his own thoughts and finds no other inspiration.

—*Pearl Buck*

One of the surest evidences of friendship that one individual can display to another is telling him gently of a fault. If any other can excel it, it is listening to such a disclosure with gratitude, and amending the error.

—*Edward Bulwer-Lytton*

Don't smother each other. No one can grow in the shade.

—*Leo Buscaglia*

I always felt that the great high privilege, relief and comfort of friendship was that one had to explain nothing.

—*Katherine Mansfield*

Friendship is like money, easier made than kept.

—*Samuel Butler*

You are forgiven for your happiness and your successes only if you generously consent to share them.

—*Albert Camus*

Love is an irresistible desire to be irresistibly desired.

—*Robert Frost*

If you want to win friends, make it a point to remember them. If you remember my name, you pay me a subtle compliment; you indicate that I have made an impression on you. Remember my name and you add to my feeling of importance.

—*Dale Carnegie*

If you would stand well with a great mind, leave him with a favorable impression of yourself; if with a little mind, leave him with a favorable impression of himself.

—*Samuel Taylor Coleridge*

You shall judge a man by his foes as well as by his friends.

—*Joseph Conrad*

As old wood is best to burn; old horses to ride; old books to read; old wine to drink; so are old friends most trusty to use.

—*Leonard Wright*

Advice from your friends is like the weather, some of it is good, some of it is bad.

—*Anonymous*

A friend is a person with whom I may be sincere. Before him, I may think aloud.

—*Ralph Waldo Emerson*

A loving heart is the truest wisdom.

—*Charles Dickens*

If I can stop one heart from breaking, If I can ease one pain, / Then my life will not have been in vain.

—*Emily Elizabeth Dickinson*

The glory of friendship is not the outstretched hand, nor the kindly smile, nor the joy of companionship; it is the spiritual inspiration that comes to one when you discover that someone else believes in you and is willing to trust you with a friendship.

—*Ralph Waldo Emerson*

One is very crazy when in love.

—*Sigmund Freud*

Love in its essence is spiritual fire.

—*Emanuel Swedenborg*

Love is a hole in the heart.

—*Ben Hecht*

Ah, when to the heart of man / Was it ever less than a treason / To go with the drift of things / To yield with a grace to reason / And bow and accept at the end / Of a love or a season.

—*Robert Frost*

Fill each other's cup but drink not from one cup.
Give one another of your bread but eat not from the same loaf.
Sing and dance together and be joyous, but let each one of you be alone,
Even as the strings of a lute are alone though they quiver with the
same music.

—*Kahlil Gibran*

A true friend is the greatest of all blessings, and that which we take the
least care of all to acquire.

—*François de La Rochefoucauld*

Friendship is born at that moment when one person says to another:
What! You, too? I thought I was the only one.

—*C. S. Lewis*

We must develop and maintain the capacity to forgive. He who is devoid
of the power to forgive is devoid of the power to love. There is some
good in the worst of us and some evil in the best of us.

—*Martin Luther King, Jr.*

Love is a canvas furnished by Nature and embroidered by imagination.

—*Voltaire*

We don't love qualities, we love persons; sometimes by reason of their defects as well as of their qualities.

—*Jacques Maritain*

The most I can do for my friend is simply to be his friend.

—*Henry David Thoreau*

Listening is a magnetic and strange thing, a creative force. The friends who listen to us are the ones we move toward. When we are listened to, it creates us, makes us unfold and expand.

—*Dr. Karl Augustus Menninger*

Faults shared are as comfortable as bedroom slippers and as easy to slip into.

—*Phyllis McGinley*

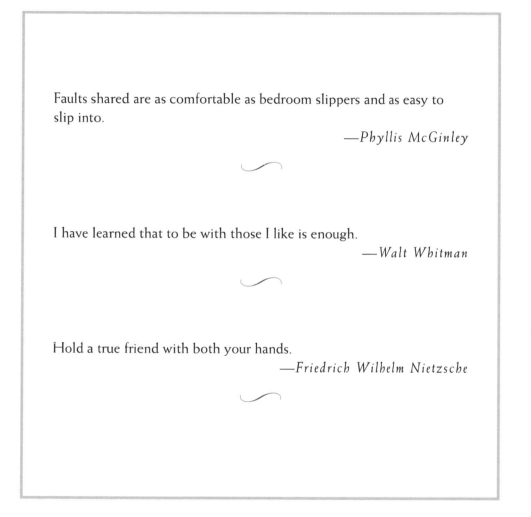

I have learned that to be with those I like is enough.

—*Walt Whitman*

Hold a true friend with both your hands.

—*Friedrich Wilhelm Nietzsche*

Absence is to love what wind is to fire; it extinguishes the small, it enkindles the great.

—*Comte Roger de Bussy-Rabutin*

A kiss is a rosy dot over the "i" of loving.

—*Cyrano de Bergerac*

Immature love says: "I love you because I need you." Mature love says "I need you because I love you."

—*Erich Fromm*

True friendship is like sound health; the value of it is seldom known until it be lost.

—*Charles Caleb Colton*

A real friend is one who walks in when the rest of the world walks out.

—*Anonymous*

Don't walk in front of me, I may not follow. Don't walk behind me, I may not lead. Walk beside me and be my friend.

—*Albert Camus*

The deepest principle in human nature is the craving to be appreciated.

—*William James*

Forget injuries, never forget kindnesses.

—*Confucius*

Kindness is more important than wisdom, and the recognition of this is the beginning of wisdom.

—*Theodore Isaac Rubin*

Tell me who your friends are and I will tell you who you are.

—*Russian proverb*

Let me not to the marriage of true minds
Admit impediments. Love is not love
Which alters when it alteration finds,
Or bends with the remover to remove.
O, no! It is an ever-fixed mark
That looks on tempests and is never shaken;
It is the star to every wand'ring bark,
Whose worth's unknown, although his height be taken.
Love's not Time's fool, though rosy lips and cheeks
Within his ending sickle's compass come;
Love alters not with his brief hours and weeks,
But bears it out even to the edge of doom.
If this be error and upon me proved,
I never writ, nor no man ever loved.

—*William Shakespeare, Sonnet 116*

Familiar acts are beautiful through love.

—*Percy Bysshe Shelley*

No man is wise enough by himself.

—*Plautus*

A friend is a present you give yourself.

—*Robert Louis Stevenson*

A friend is someone who can sing you the song of your heart when you've forgotten it.

—*Anonymous*

The greatest good you can do for another is not just to share your riches but to reveal to him his own.

—*Benjamin Disraeli*

Tis better to have loved and lost / Than never to have loved at all.

—*Alfred, Lord Tennyson*

We cannot all do great things, but we can do small things with great love.

—*Mother Teresa*

To love and win is the best thing. To love and lose, the next best.

—*William Makepeace Thackeray*

My friend is one who takes me for what I am.

—*Henry David Thoreau*

III

SUCCESS

and Ways to Achieve It

Success is the ability to go from one failure to another with no loss of enthusiasm.

—*Sir Winston Churchill*

The obstacle is the path.

—*Zen aphorism*

You have brains in your head
You have feet in your shoes
You can steer yourself
any direction you choose
You're on your own. And you know what you know.
And YOU are the guy who'll decide where to go.

—*Dr. Seuss (Theodore Geisel)*

Genius is one percent inspiration and ninty-nine percent perspiration.

—*Thomas Alva Edison*

It is not enough to be busy. . . . The question is: what are we busy about?

—*Henry David Thoreau*

The indispensable first step to getting the things you want out of life is this: Decide what you want.

—*Ben Stein*

All good things which exist are the fruits of originality.

—*John Stuart Mill*

The person who makes a success of living is the one who sees his goal steadily and aims for it unswervingly.

—*Cecil B. DeMille*

The best way to make your dreams come true is to wake up.

—*Paul Valéry*

In the field of observation, chance favors the prepared mind.

—*Louis Pasteur*

The future belongs to those who believe in the beauty of their dreams.

—*Eleanor Roosevelt*

Things turn out best for the people who make the best of the way things turn out.

—*John R. Wooden*

Any activity becomes creative when the doer cares about doing it right, or better.

—*John Updike*

Eighty percent of success is just showing up.

—*Woody Allen*

Be wiser than other people, if you can; but do not tell them so.
—*Philip Dormer Stanhope, Lord Chesterfield*

No illusion is more crucial than the illusion that great success and huge money buy you immunity from the common ills of mankind, such as cars that won't start.

—*Larry McMurtry*

When in doubt, win the trick.

—*Edmond Hoyle*

There is only one boss: the customer. And he can fire everybody in the company, from the chairman on down, simply by spending his money somewhere else.

—*Sam Walton*

If it be now, 'tis not to come; if it be not to come, it will be
now; if it be not now, yet it will come: the readiness is all.

—*William Shakespeare*

The secret of successful managing is to keep the five guys who hate you
away from the four guys who haven't made up their minds.

—*Charles "Casey" Stengel*

Measure twice, cut once.

—*Craftsman's aphorism*

Take calculated risks. That is quite different from being rash.

—*George Smith Patton, Jr.*

In reading the lives of great men, I found that the first victory they won was over themselves . . . self-discipline with all of them came first.

—*Harry S. Truman*

Never think that you're not good enough yourself. A man should never think that. People will take you very much at your own reckoning.

—*Anthony Trollope*

There are two things to aim at in life: first, to get what you want; and, after that, to enjoy it. Only the wisest of mankind achieve the second.

—*Logan Pearsall Smith*

It is necessary for us to learn from others' mistakes. You will not live long enough to make them all yourself.

—*Hyman George Rickover*

A wise man sees as much as he ought, not as much as he can.

—*Michel de Montaigne*

Without leaps of imagination, or dreaming, we lose the excitement of possibilities. Dreaming, after all, is a form of planning.

—*Gloria Steinem*

The man who trims himself to suit everybody will soon whittle himself away.

—*Charles Schwab*

The dreadful burden of having nothing to do.

—*Nicolas Boileau*

Some people believe that holding on and hanging in there are signs of great strength. However, there are times when it takes much more strength to know when to let go—and then do it.

—*Ann Landers*

The greater danger for most of us lies not in setting our aim too high and falling short, but in setting our aim too low, and achieving our mark.

—*Michelangelo*

The cure for boredom is curiosity. There is no cure for curiosity.

—*Ellen Parr*

With self-discipline most anything is possible.

—*Theodore Roosevelt*

I don't know the key to success, but the key to failure is trying to please everybody.

—*Bill Cosby*

I always tried to turn every disaster into an opportunity.

—*John D. Rockefeller, Jr.*

He who does not risk will never drink champagne.

—*Russian proverb*

Ability is sexless.

—*John Henry Newman*

For most of history, Anonymous was a woman.

—*Virginia Woolf*

Fortune favors the brave.

—*Terence*

I'm a great believer in luck, and I find the harder I work the more I have of it.

—Thomas Jefferson

One of the advantages of being disorderly is that one is constantly making exciting discoveries.

—A. A. Milne

The bravest are surely those who have the clearest vision of what is before them, glory and danger alike, and yet notwithstanding go out to meet it.

—Thucydides

Never let your head hang down. Never give up and sit down and grieve. Find another way. And don't pray when it rains if you don't pray when the sun shines.

—*Satchel Paige*

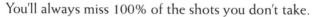

You'll always miss 100% of the shots you don't take.

—*Wayne Gretzky*

There is hardly anything in the world that some man can't make a little worse and sell a little cheaper, and the people who consider price only are this man's lawful prey.

—*John Ruskin*

Oh, the tangled webs we weave / When we practice to deceive.

—Sir Walter Scott

Nothing is a waste of time if you use the experience wisely.

—Auguste Rodin

What lies behind us and what lies before us are tiny matters compared to what lies within us.

—Ralph Waldo Emerson

Work expands to fill the time available for its completion.

—Cyril Northcote Parkinson

(known as Parkinson's Law)

If anything can go wrong, it will.

—Murphy's Law

(named after Air Force Captain Edward A. Murphy, an engineer working on a
project to see how much sudden deceleration a human can stand in a crash)

I have not failed. I've just found 10,000 ways that won't work.

—Thomas Alva Edison

Formula for success: Underpromise and overdeliver.

—Thomas Peters

The best way to escape from a problem is to solve it.

—Anonymous

A creative man is motivated by the desire to achieve, not by the desire to beat others.

—Ayn Rand

Know from whence you came. If you know whence you came, there are absolutely no limitations to where you can go.

—*James Baldwin*

There is no disinfectant like success.

—*Daniel J. Boorstin*

Nothing succeeds like success.

—*Alexander Dumas*

What is harder than rock, or softer than water? Yet soft water hollows out hard rock. Persevere.

—Ovid

Prosperity is a great teacher; adversity a greater.

—William Hazlitt

If I have seen further than others, it is by standing upon the shoulders of giants.

—Sir Isaac Newton

The spirit, the will to win, and the will to excel are the things that endure. These qualities are so much more important than the events that occur.

—*Vince Lombardi*

One of the lessons of history is that nothing is often a good thing to do and always a clever thing to say.

—*Will Durant*

It takes less time to do a thing right, than it does to explain why you did it wrong.

—*Henry Wadsworth Longfellow*

The speed of a runaway horse counts for nothing.

—*Jean Cocteau*

No one ever gets far unless he accomplishes the impossible at least once a day.

—*L. Ron Hubbard*

Perfection is achieved, not when there is nothing left to add, but when there is nothing left to take away.

—*Antoine de Saint-Exupéry*

It is true greatness to have in one the frailty of a man and the security of a god.

—*Lucius Annaeus Seneca*

Success is how high you bounce when you hit bottom.

—*George Smith Patton, Jr.*

A bank is a place where they lend you an umbrella in fair weather and ask for it back when it begins to rain.

—*Robert Frost*

We often discover what will do, by finding out what will not do; and probably he who never made a mistake never made a discovery.

—*Samuel Smiles*

One thing life taught me: if you are interested, you never have to look for new interests. They come to you. When you are genuinely interested in one thing, it will always lead to something else.

—*Eleanor Roosevelt*

To do good thing in the world, first you must know who you are and what gives meaning to your life.

—*Robert Browning*

You just don't luck into things as much as you'd like to think you do. You build step by step, whether it's friendships or opportunities.

—*Barbara Bush*

Whether you think you can or whether you think you can't, you're right.

—*Henry Ford*

An inconvenience is only an adventure wrongly considered; an adventure is an inconvenience rightly considered.

—*G. K. Chesterton*

It is the part of a wise man to keep himself to-day for to-morrow, and not to venture all his eggs in one basket.

—*Miguel de Cervantes*

To please everybody is impossible; were I to undertake it, I should probably please nobody.

—*George Washington*

During my eighty-seven years I have witnessed a whole succession of technological revolutions. But none of them has done away with the need for character in the individual or the ability to think.

—*Bernard Mannes Baruch*

When clouds form in the skies we know that rain will follow but we must not wait for it. Nothing will be achieved by attempting to interfere with the future before the time is ripe. Patience is needed.

—*I Ching*

Keep away from people who try to belittle your ambitions. Small people always do that, but the really great make you feel that you too, can become great.

—*Mark Twain*

A good solution applied with vigor now is better than a perfect solution applied ten minutes later.

—*George Smith Patton, Jr.*

Being a hero is about the shortest-lived profession on earth.

—*Will Rogers*

One day Alice came to a fork in the road and saw a Cheshire cat in a tree. "Which road do I take?" she asked. "Where do you want to go?" was his response. "I don't know," Alice answered. "Then," said the cat, "it doesn't matter."

—*Lewis Carroll*

Spoon feeding in the long run teaches us nothing but the shape of the spoon.

—*E. M. Forster*

If I have ever made any valuable discoveries, it has been owing more to patient attention, than to any other talent.

—*Sir Isaac Newton*

If a man will begin with certainties, he shall end in doubts; but if he will be content to begin with doubts he shall end in certainties.

—*Sir Francis Bacon*

I not only use all the brains that I have, but all that I can borrow.

—*Woodrow Wilson*

They say that time changes things, but you actually have to change them yourself.

—*Andy Warhol*

It is a paradoxical but profoundly true and important principle of life that the most likely way to reach a goal is to be aiming not at that goal itself but at some more ambitious goal beyond it.

—*Arnold Joseph Toynbee*

It is a bad plan that admits of no modification.

—*Publilius Syrus*

It takes as much energy to wish as it does to plan.

—*Eleanor Roosevelt*

One of the annoying things about believing in free will and individual responsibility is the difficulty of finding somebody to blame your problems on. And when you do find somebody, it's remarkable how often his picture turns up on your driver's license.

—*P. J. O'Rourke*

Who dares, wins.

—*Anonymous*

It does not matter how slowly you go so long as you do not stop.

—*Confucius*

I learned much from my teachers, more from my books, and most from my mistakes.

—*Anonymous*

A wise man will make more opportunities than he finds.

—*Sir Francis Bacon*

If the only tool you have is a hammer, every problem looks like a nail.

—*Abraham Maslow*

Next to knowing when to seize an opportunity, the next important thing is to know when to forego an advantage.

—*Benjamin Disraeli*

Lead, follow, or get out of the way.

—*Thomas Paine*

The manner in which a man chooses to gamble indicates his character or his lack of it.

—*William Saroyan*

If you wish in this world to advance,
Your merits you're bound to enhance;
You must stir it and stump it,
and blow your own trumpet.
Or trust me, you haven't a chance.

—*Sir William S. Gilbert*

Leadership is solving problems. The day soldiers stop bringing you their problems is the day you have stopped leading them. They have either lost confidence that you can help or concluded you do not care. Either case is a failure of leadership.

—*Colin Powell*

You can't always get what you want / But if you try sometime you might find / You get what you need.

—*Mick Jagger and Keith Richards*

Success is dependent on effort.

—*Sophocles*

People cannot be managed. Inventories can be managed, but people must be led.

—*H. Ross Perot*

If you believe you can, you probably can. If you believe you won't, you most assuredly won't. Belief is the ignition switch that gets you off the launching pad.

—*Denis Waitley*

It doesn't matter if a cat is black or white, so long as it catches mice.

—*Deng Xiaoping*

A good objective of leadership is to help those who are doing poorly to do well and to help those who are doing well to do even better.

—*Jim Rohn*

Clear your mind of can't.

—Solon

Giving your son a skill is better than giving him one thousand pieces of gold.

—Chinese proverb

. . . Give every man thy ear, but few thy voice;
Take each man's censure, but reserve thy judgment.
Costly thy habit as thy purse can buy . . .
Neither a borrower nor a lender be;
For loan oft loses both itself and friend,
And borrowing dulls the edge of husbandry.

—William Shakespeare

There is no such thing as a "self-made" person. . . . Everyone who has ever done a kind deed for us, or spoken one word of encouragement to us, has entered into the make-up of our character and of our thoughts, as well as our success.

—*George Matthew Adams*

Difficulty, my brethren, is the nurse of greatness—a harsh nurse, who roughly rocks her foster-children into strength and athletic proportion.

—*William Cullen Bryant*

If nothing ever changed, there'd be no butterflies.

—*Anonymous*

Progress, far from consisting in change, depends on retentiveness. When change is absolute there remains no being to improve and no direction is set for possible improvement: and when experience is not retained, as among savages, infancy is perpetual. Those who cannot remember the past are condemned to repeat it.

—*George Santayana*

The man who has no imagination has no wings.

—*Muhammad Ali*

I love the man that can smile in trouble, that can gather strength from distress, and grow brave by reflection. 'Tis the business of little minds to shrink, but he whose heart is firm, and whose conscience approves his conduct, will pursue his principles unto death.

—*Thomas Paine*

I try to do the right thing at the right time. They may just be little things, but usually they make the difference between winning and losing.

—*Kareem Abdul-Jabar*

Great deeds are usually wrought at great risks.

—*Herodotus*

Prosperity depends more on wanting what you have than having what you want.

—*Geoffrey F. Abert*

If it sounds too good to be true, it is.

—*Anonymous*

Never esteem anything as of advantage to you that will make you break your word or lose your self-respect.

—*Henry Brooks Adams*

If you're not failing every now and again, it's a sign you're not doing anything very innovative.

—*Woody Allen*

If you don't like something change it. If you can't change it, change your attitude. Don't complain.

—*Maya Angelou*

We are what we repeatedly do, Excellence is therefore not an act but a habit.

—*Aristotle*

Never play cards with a man called Doc, never eat at a place called Mom's, and never sleep with a woman whose troubles are worse than your own.

—*Nelson Algren*

Less is more.

—*Ludwig Mies van der Rohe*

All things are difficult before they are easy.

—*Thomas Fuller*

It is not always by plugging away at a difficulty and sticking at it that one overcomes it; but, rather, often by working on the one next to it. Certain people and certain things require to be approached on an angle.

—*Matthew Arnold*

A subtle thought that is in error may yet give rise to fruitful inquiry that can establish truths of great value.

—*Isaac Asimov*

If money be not thy servant, it will be thy master. The covetous man cannot so properly be said to possess wealth, as that may be said to possess him.

—*Sir Francis Bacon*

One of the things I learned the hard way was that it doesn't pay to get discouraged. Keeping busy and making optimism a way of life can restore your faith in yourself.

—*Lucille Ball*

In a hierarchy every employee tends to rise to his level of incompetence.
—*Laurence J. Peter*
(expressing the so-called Peter Principle)

Those who know how to win are more numerous than those who know how to make proper use of their victories.
—*Polybius*

Power is not revealed by striking hard or often, but by striking true.
—*Honoré de Balzac*

Millions saw the apple fall, but Newton was the one who asked why.

—*Bernard Baruch*

It's what you learn after you know it all that's important.

—*Jimmy Williams*

Call it what you will, incentives are what get people to work harder.

—*Nikita Khruschev*

What makes a good follower? The single most important characteristic may well be a willingness to tell the truth. In a world of growing complexity leaders are increasingly dependent on their subordinates for good information, whether the leaders want to hear it or not. Followers who tell the truth and leaders who listen to it are an unbeatable combination.

—*Warren G. Bennis*

Riches do not consist in the possession of treasures, but in the use made of them.

—*Napoléon Bonaparte*

The best computer is a man, and it's the only one that can be mass-produced by unskilled labor.

—*Wernher von Braun*

A hunch is creativity trying to tell you something.

—*Frank Capra*

Any fool can make things bigger, more complex, and more violent. It takes a touch of genius—and a lot of courage—to move in the opposite direction.

—*Albert Einstein*

The person interested in success has to learn to view failure as a healthy, inevitable part of the process of getting to the top.

—*Dr. Joyce Brothers*

Good judgment comes from experience, and experience usually comes from bad judgment.

—*Anonymous*

Ah, but a man's reach should exceed his grasp—or what's a heaven for?

—*Robert Browning*

The way to develop self-confidence is to do the thing you fear and get a record of successful experiences behind you. Destiny is not a matter of chance, it is a matter of choice; it is not a thing to be waited for, it is a thing to be achieved.

—*William Jennings Bryan*

Believe nothing merely because you have been told it. Do not believe what your teacher tells you merely out of respect for the teacher. But whatsoever, after due examination and analysis, you find to be kind, conducive to the good, the benefit, the welfare of all beings—that doctrine believe and cling to, and take it as your guide.

—Buddha

You can do very little with faith, but you can do nothing without it.

—Samuel Butler

When you follow your bliss . . . doors will open where you would not have thought there would be doors; and where there wouldn't be a door for anyone else.

—Joseph Campbell

The truth that many people never understand, until it is too late, is that the more you try to avoid suffering the more you suffer because smaller and more insignificant things begin to torture you in proportion to your fear of being hurt.

—*Thomas Merton*

You can get a lot farther with a kind word and a gun than a kind word alone.

—*Al Capone*

The man without a purpose is like a ship without a rudder—a waif, a nothing, a no man. Have a purpose in life and having it, throw such strength of mind and muscle into your work as God has given you.

—*Thomas Carlyle*

"Where shall I begin, please, your Majesty?" he asked.
"Begin at the beginning," the King said, gravely, "and go on till you come to the end: then stop."

—*Lewis Carroll*

Perseverance alone does not assure success. No amount of stalking will lead to game in a field that has none.

—*I Ching*

For myself I am an optimist—it does not seem to be much use being anything else.

—*Sir Winston Churchill*

Nothing in the world can take the place of persistence. Talent will not; nothing is more common than unsuccessful men with talent. Genius will not; unrewarded genius is almost a proverb. Education will not; the world is full of educated derelicts. Persistence and determination are omnipotent.

—Calvin Coolidge

Iron rusts from disuse; stagnant water loses it purity and in cold weather becomes frozen; even so does inaction sap the vigor of the mind.

—Leonardo da Vinci

Believe those who are seeking the truth; doubt those who find it.

—André Gide

The only safe thing is to take a chance. Play safe and you are dead. Taking risks is the essence of good work, and the difference between safe and bold can only be defined by yourself since no one else knows for what you are hoping when you embark on anything.

—*Mike Nichols*

Sometimes you have to play for a long time to be able to play like yourself.

—*Miles Davis, Jr.*

It is a common experience that a problem difficult at night is resolved in the morning after a committee of sleep has worked on it.

—*John Steinbeck*

Small opportunities are often the beginning of great enterprises.

—*Demosthenes*

If you're not making mistakes, you're not trying hard enough.

—*Vince Lombardi*

Failure is instructive. The person who really thinks learns quite as much from his failures as from his successes.

—*John Dewey*

Luck is the residue of design.

—*Branch Rickey*

Speak the truth, do not yield to anger; give, if thou art asked for little; by these three steps thou wilt go near the gods.

—*The Dhammapada*

Nothing can be produced out of nothing.

—*Diogenes Läertius*

When you have eliminated the impossible, that which remains, however improbable, must be the truth.

—*Sir Arthur Conan Doyle*

You can't build a reputation on what you're going to do.

—*Henry Ford*

The winds and the waves are always on the side of the ablest navigators.

—*Edward Gibbon*

Annual income twenty pounds, annual expenditure nineteen pounds and six, result happiness. Annual income twenty pounds, annual expenditure twenty pounds ought and six, result misery.

—*Charles Dickens*

Don't accept your dog's admiration as conclusive evidence that you are wonderful.

—*Ann Landers*

Nothing great was ever achieved without enthusiasm.

—*Ralph Waldo Emerson*

The world is full of willing people; some willing to work, the rest willing to let them.

—*Robert Frost*

I respect the man who knows distinctly what he wishes. The greater part of all mischief in the world arises from the fact that men do not sufficiently understand their own aims. They have undertaken to build a tower, and spend no more labor on the foundation than would be necessary to erect a hut.

—*Johann Wolfgang von Goethe*

You cannot play with the animal in you without becoming wholly animal, play with falsehood without forfeiting your right to truth, play with cruelty without losing your sensitivity of mind. He who wants to keep his garden tidy doesn't reserve a plot for weeds.

—*Dag Hammarskjöld*

My weakness has always been to prefer the large intention of an unskill-
ful artist to the trivial intention of an accomplished one: in other words,
I am more interested in the high ideas of a feeble executant than in the
high execution of a feeble thinker.

—Thomas Hardy

I have the simplest tastes. I am always satisfied with the best.

—Oscar Wilde

We are wiser than we know.

—Ralph Waldo Emerson

Happiness is as a butterfly which, when pursued, is always beyond our grasp, but which if you will sit down quietly, may alight upon you.

—*Nathaniel Hawthorne*

There is a tide in the affairs of men,
Which taken at the flood, leads on to fortune;
Omitted, all the voyage of their life
Is bound in shallows and in miseries.

—*William Shakespeare*

I find the great thing in this world is not so much where we stand, as in what direction we are moving—we must sail sometimes with the wind and sometimes against it—but we must sail, and not drift, nor lie at anchor.

—*Oliver Wendell Holmes, Jr.*

I have had dreams and I have had nightmares, but I have conquered my nightmares because of my dreams.

—*Jonas Salk*

Trifles make perfections, but perfection is itself no trifle.

—*Shaker proverb*

Success without honor is an unseasoned dish; it will satisfy your hunger, but it won't taste good.

—*Joe Paterno*

Experience is not what happens to you, it is what you do with what happens to you.

—*Aldous Huxley*

Nothing is built on stone; all is built on sand, but we must build as if the sand were stone.

—*Jorge Luis Borges*

A man must be big enough to admit his mistakes, smart enough to profit from them, and strong enough to correct them.

—*John C. Maxwell*

Nothing will ever be attempted if all possible objections must first be overcome.

—Samuel Johnson

There is only one success—to be able to spend your life in your own way.

—Christopher Darlington Morley

The most pathetic person in the world is someone who has sight, but has no vision.

—Helen Keller

You ain't gonna learn what you don't wanna know.

—Jerry Garcia

If I were asked to give what I consider the single most useful bit of advice for all humanity, it would be this: Expect trouble as an inevitable part of life. . . . Look it squarely in the eye, and say, I will be bigger than you. You cannot defeat me.

—Ann Landers

If men could regard the events of their own lives with more open minds, they would frequently discover that they did not really desire the things they failed to obtain.

—André Maurois

The highest reward for a man's toil is not what he gets for it but what he becomes by it.

—John Ruskin

Practice doesn't make perfect. Perfect practice makes perfect.

—Vince Lombardi

It takes as much stress to be a success as it does to be a failure.

—Emilio James Trujillo

In the fight between you and the world, back the world.

—*Franz Kafka*

There is always an easy solution to every human problem—neat, plausible, and wrong.

—*H. L. Mencken*

Imagination will often carry us to worlds that never were. But without it we go nowhere.

—*Carl Sagan*

A timid person is frightened before a danger, a coward during the time, and a courageous person afterward.

—*Jean Paul Friedrich Richter*

A habit cannot be tossed out the window; it must be coaxed down the stairs a step at a time.

—*Mark Twain*

Mishaps are like knives, that either serve us or cut us, as we grasp them by the blade or the handle.

—*James Russell Lowell*

The two most powerful warriors are patience and time.

—Leo Tolstoy

The greatest glory in living lies not in never falling, but in rising every time we fall.

—Nelson Mandela

Everybody knows if you are too careful you are so occupied in being careful that you are sure to stumble over something.

—Gertrude Stein

A professional is a man who can do his best at a time when he doesn't particularly feel like it.

—*Alistair Cooke*

The man who can drive himself further once the effort gets painful is the man who will win.

—*Roger Bannister*

Do continue to believe that with your feeling and your work you are taking part in the greatest; the more strongly you cultivate this belief, the more will reality and the world go forth from it.

—*Rainer Maria Rilke*

Doing the best at this moment puts you in the best place for the next moment.

—*Oprah Winfrey*

There are no menial jobs, only menial attitudes.

—*William John Bennett*

Mistakes are the portals for discovery.

—*James Joyce*

The pupil who is never required to do what he cannot do, never does what he can do.

—*John Stuart Mill*

     . . . God doth not need
Either man's work or his own gifts; who best
Bear his mild yoke, they serve him best; his State
is Kingly. Thousands at his bidding speed
And post o'er Land and Ocean without rest:
They also serve who only stand and wait.

—*John Milton*

Never tell people how to do things. Tell them what you want them to achieve, and they will surprise you with their ingenuity.

—*George Smith Patton, Jr.*

There are two kinds of failures: those who thought and never did, and those who did and never thought.

—*Laurence J. Peter*

Obstacles are those frightful things you see when you take your eyes off your goal.

—*Henry Ford*

Problems are only opportunities in work clothes.

—*Henry J. Kaiser*

Use what talents you possess: the woods would be very silent if no birds sang there except those that sang best.

—*Henry Van Dyke*

Success usually comes to those who are too busy to be looking for it.

—*Henry David Thoreau*

I would rather fail in a cause that will ultimately triumph than to triumph in cause that will ultimately fail.

—*Woodrow Wilson*

One should not increase, beyond what is necessary, the number of entities required to explain anything.

—*William of Occam*

(this principle of parsimony is known as "Occam's razor")

When I am working on a problem, I never think about beauty . . . but when I have finished, if the solution is not beautiful, I know it is wrong.

—*R. Buckminster Fuller*

Merely having an open mind is nothing; the object of opening the mind, as of opening the mouth, is to shut it again on something solid.

—*G. K. Chesterton*

Blessed is the man who, having nothing to say, abstains from giving us wordy evidence of the fact.

—*George Eliot*

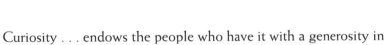

Curiosity . . . endows the people who have it with a generosity in argument and a serenity in cheerful willingness to let life take the form it will.

—*Alistair Cooke*

Ideas won't keep; something must be done about them.

—*Alfred North Whitehead*

When people keep telling you that you can't do a thing, you kind of like to try it.

—*Margaret Chase Smith*

Never grow a wishbone where your backbone ought to be.

—*Clementine Paddleford*

Nobody can make you feel inferior without your consent.

—*Eleanor Roosevelt*

Kind words are short and easy to speak, but their echoes are
truly endless.

—*Mother Teresa*

Commit yourself to a dream. . . . Nobody who tries to do something
great but fails is a total failure. Why? Because he can always rest assured
that he succeeded in life's most important battle—he defeated the fear of
trying.

—*Robert H. Schuller*

You can be discouraged by failure—or you can learn from it. So go ahead
and make mistakes. Make all you can. Because, remember that's where
you'll find success. On the far side.

—*Thomas Watson, Sr.*

I am always doing that which I can not do, in order that I may learn how to do it.

—*Pablo Picasso*

Always do sober what you said you'd do drunk. That will teach you to keep your mouth shut

—*Ernest Hemingway*

There is nothing more difficult to take in hand, more perilous to conduct, or more uncertain in its success, than to take the lead in the introduction of a new order to things.

—*Niccolò Machiavelli*

Diamonds are nothing more than chunks of coal that stuck to their jobs.

—*Malcolm Forbes*

Ambition can creep as well as soar.

—*Edmund Burke*

If we work upon marble, it will perish; if we work upon brass, time will efface it; if we rear temples, they will crumble into dust; but if we work upon immortal minds and instill into them just principles, we are then engraving that upon tablets which no time will efface, but will brighten and brighten to all eternity.

—*Daniel Webster*

The best leaders of all are ones the people do not know exist. They turn to each other and say we did it ourselves.

—Zen aphorism

They can do all because they think they can.

—Virgil

White. A blank page or canvas. So many possibilities.

—Stephen Sondheim

We're all proud of making little mistakes. It gives us the feeling we don't make any big ones.

—Andy Rooney

People have been known to achieve more as a result of working with others than against them.

—Dr. Allan Fromme

Four things come not back: the spoken word, the spent arrow, the past, the neglected opportunity.

—Omar Ibn Al-Halif

Anywhere is walking distance, if you've got the time.

—*Steven Wright*

A jest's prosperity lies in the ear of him that hears it, never in the tongue of him that makes it.

—*William Shakespeare*

Trust yourself. You know more than you think you do.

—*Benjamin Spock*

I would sooner fail than not be among the greatest.

—John Keats

For everything you have missed, you have gained something else.

—Ralph Waldo Emerson

If you don't make a total commitment to whatever you're doing, then you start looking to bail out the first time the boat starts leaking. It's tough enough getting that boat to shore with everybody rowing, let alone when a guy stands up and starts putting his jacket on.

—Lou Holtz

When you reach for the stars, you may not quite get them, but you won't come up with a handful of mud either.

—*Leo Burnett*

When the will defies fear, when the heart applauds the brain, when duty throws the gauntlet down to fate, when honor scorns to compromise with death—this is heroism.

—*Robert Ingersoll*

Let fear be a counselor and not a jailer.

—*Anthony Robbins*

Envy, among other ingredients, has a mixture of love of justice in it. We are more angry at undeserved than at deserved good fortune.

—William Hazlitt

Things don't change, but by and by our wishes change.

—Marcel Proust

Having once decided to achieve a certain task, achieve it at all cost of tedium and distaste. The gain in self-confidence of having accomplished a tiresome labor is immense.

—Arnold Bennett

He who desires but acts not, breeds pestilence.

—*William Blake*

~

The artist is nothing without the gift, but the gift is nothing without work.

—*Émile Zola*

~

God gave us our memories so that we might have roses in December.

—*Sir James Matthew Barrie*

~

No artist is ahead of his time. He is his time. It is just that the others are behind the time.

—*Martha Graham*

You can never step into the same river twice; for new waters are always flowing on to you.

—*Heraclitus*

A work is perfectly finished only when nothing can be added to it and nothing taken away.

—*Joseph Joubert*

Silence is the true friend that never betrays.

—*Confucius*

How often misused words generate misleading thoughts.

—*Herbert Spencer*

Beware the fury of a patient man!

—*John Dryden*

A ship in harbor is safe, but that is not what ships are built for.

—*John A. Shedd*

What counts is not necessarily the size of the dog in the fight—it's the size of the fight in the dog.

—*Dwight D. Eisenhower*

Be like the promotory against which the waves continually break, but it stands firm and tames the fury of the water around it.

—*Marcus Aurelius*

Never mistake motion for action.

—*Ernest Hemingway*

The reward of a thing well done is to have done it.

—*Ralph Waldo Emerson*

Advice is like snow; the softer it falls the longer it dwells upon, and the deeper it sinks into the mind.

—*Samuel Taylor Coleridge*

You don't need a weather man / To know which way the wind blows.

—*Bob Dylan*

You trust your mother, but you cut the cards.

—*Anonymous*

When you reach the top, keep climbing.

—*Zen aphorism*

You can observe a lot just by watching.

—*Yogi Berra*

My father [President Franklin D. Roosevelt] gave me these hints on speech-making: be sincere . . . be brief . . . be seated.

—*James Roosevelt*

You've got to take the initiative and play your game. In a decisive set, confidence is the difference.

—*Chris Evert*

The codfish lays ten thousand eggs, the homely hen lays one. / The codfish never cackles to tell you what she's done. / And so we scorn the codfish, while the humble hen we prize, / which only goes to show you that it pays to advertise.

—*Anonymous*

All human wisdom is summed up in two words—wait and hope.

—*Alexander Dumas*

To laugh often and much; to win the respect of intelligent people and the affection of children; to earn the appreciation of honest critics and endure the betrayal of false friends; to appreciate beauty, to find the best in others; to leave the world a little better; whether by a healthy child, a garden patch or a redeemed social condition; to know even one life has breathed easier because you have lived. This is the meaning of success.

—*Ralph Waldo Emerson*

THE LIFE
OF THE
MIND

Cogito ergo sum. (I think, therefore I am.)

—René Descartes

Nothing else in the world . . . not all the armies . . . is so powerful as an idea whose time has come.

—Victor Hugo

We are shaped by our thoughts. We become what we think.

—Buddha

I'd rather learn from one bird how to sing than to teach ten thousand stars how not to dance.

—*e. e. cummings*

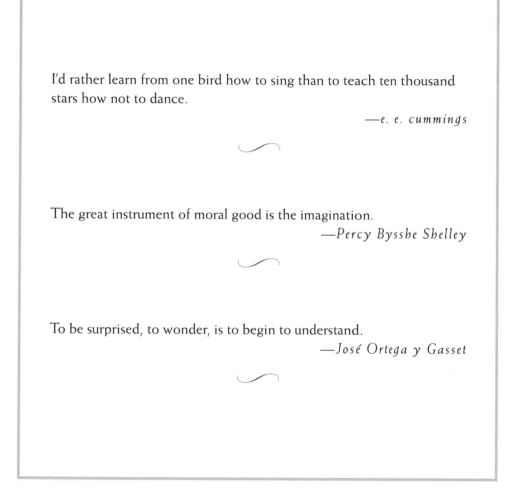

The great instrument of moral good is the imagination.

—*Percy Bysshe Shelley*

To be surprised, to wonder, is to begin to understand.

—*José Ortega y Gasset*

Knowledge is power.

—Sir Francis Bacon

It is impossible to defeat an ignorant man in argument.

—William G. McAdoo

I am the wisest man alive, for I know one thing, and that is that I know nothing.

—Socrates

Knowledge can be conveyed, but not wisdom. It can be found, it can be lived, it is possible to be carried by it, miracles can be performed with it, but it cannot be expressed in words and taught.

—*Herman Hesse*

Skepticism is the chastity of the intellect, and it is shameful to surrender it too soon or to the first comer: there is nobility in preserving it coolly and proudly through long youth, until at last, in the ripeness of instinct and discretion, it can be safely exchanged for fidelity and happiness.

—*George Santayana*

Others have been here before me, and I walk in their footsteps. The books I have read were composed by generations of fathers and sons, mothers and daughters, teachers and disciples. I am the sum total of their experiences, their quests. And so are you.

—*Elie Wiesel*

If we value the pursuit of knowledge, we must be free to follow wherever that search may lead us. The free mind is no barking dog to be tethered on a one-foot chain.

—*Theodor Adorno*

The test of a first-rate intelligence is the ability to hold two opposed ideas in the mind at the same time, and still retain the ability to function. One should, for example, be able to see that things are hopeless and yet be determined to make them otherwise.

—*F. Scott Fitzgerald*

It is the mark of an educated mind to be able to entertain a thought without accepting it.

—*Aristotle*

Humor is a serious thing. I like to think of it as one of our greatest earliest natural resources, which must be preserved at all cost.

—James Thurber

When you read a classic you do not see in the book more than you did before. You see more in you than there was before.

—Clifton Fadiman

Mediocrity knows nothing higher than itself, but talent instantly recognizes genius.

—Sir Arthur Conan Doyle

Life beats down and crushes the soul, but art reminds you that you have one.

—*Stella Adler*

I do not feel obliged to believe that that same God who has endowed us with sense, reason, and intellect has intended us to forego their use.

—*Galileo Galilei*

Exuberance is beauty.

—*William Blake*

Writing is a struggle against silence.

—*Carlos Fuentes*

Talk sense to a fool and he calls you foolish.

—*Euripides*

Education is not the filling of a pail, but the lighting of a fire.

—*William Butler Yeats*

You cannot teach a man anything; you can only help him find it within himself.

—*Galileo Galilei*

I have always thought the actions of men the best interpreters of their thoughts.

—*John Locke*

Perhaps the most valuable result of all education is the ability to make yourself do the thing you have to do, when it ought to be done, whether you like it or not.

—*Walter Bagehot*

People demand freedom of speech to make up for the freedom of thought which they avoid.

—*Søren Kierkegaard*

Anyone who conducts an argument by appealing to authority is not using his intelligence; he is just using his memory.

—*Leonardo da Vinci*

Where so many hours have been spent in convincing myself that I am right, is there not some reason to fear I may be wrong?

—*Jane Austen*

Prejudices, it is well known, are most difficult to eradicate from the heart whose soil has never been loosened or fertilized by education; they grow there, firm as weeds among rocks.

—*Charlotte Brontë*

The test and the use of man's education is that he finds pleasure in the exercise of his mind.

—*Jacques Martin Barzun*

I find that a great part of the information I have was acquired by looking up something and finding something else on the way.

—*Franklin P. Adams*

The writer wants to be understood much more than he wants to be respected or praised or even loved. And that perhaps, is what makes him different from others.

—*Leo C. Rosten*

Fantasy, abandoned by reason, produces impossible monsters; united with it, she is the mother of the arts and the origin of marvels.

—*Francisco de Goya*

Paradoxically though it may seem, it is none the less true that life imitates art far more than art imitates life.

—*Oscar Wilde*

Genius is nothing but a great aptitude for patience.
—*George-Louis de Buffon*

People are always so boring when they band together. You have to be alone to develop all the idiosyncrasies that make a person interesting.
—*Andy Warhol*

Creative minds have been known to survive any sort of bad training.
—*Anna Freud*

An intellectual is a man who says a simple thing in a difficult way; an artist is a man who says a difficult thing in a simple way.

—*Charles Bukowski*

Conception, my boy, fundamental brain work, is what makes all the difference in art. The job of the artist is always to deepen the mystery.

—*Francis Bacon*

Art is made to disturb. Science reassures. There is only one valuable thing in art: the thing you cannot explain.

—*Georges Braque*

Precision is not reality

—*Henri Matisse*

Life is brief, art is long.

—*Hippocrates*

The purpose of art is to lay bare the questions which have been hidden by the answers.

—*James Baldwin*

The invariable mark of wisdom is to see the miraculous in the common.
—*Ralph Waldo Emerson*

Poor is the pupil who does not surpass his master.
—*Leonardo da Vinci*

Lord, grant that I may always desire more than I can accomplish.
—*Michelangelo*

Creativity is allowing yourself to make mistakes. Art is knowing which ones to keep.

—*Scott Adams*

In every man's heart there is a secret nerve that answers to the vibrations of beauty.

—*Christopher Darlington Morley*

Beauty in things lies in the mind which contemplates them.

—*David Hume*

The best and most beautiful things in life cannot be seen, not touched, but are felt in the heart.

—*Helen Keller*

There are flowers everywhere, for those who bother to look.

—*Henri Matisse*

God, give us the grace to accept with serenity the things that cannot be changed, courage to change the things which should be changed, and the wisdom to distinguish the one from the other.

—*Reinhold Niebuhr*

Do not say a little in many words but a great deal in a few.

—*Pythagorus*

What sculpture is to a block of marble, education is to the soul.

—*Joseph Addison*

Real education should educate us out of self into something far finer; into a selflessness which links us with all humanity.

—*Lady Nancy Astor*

To educate a man is to unfit him to be a slave.

—*Fredrick Douglass*

No man can be called friendless when he has God and the companion-ship of good books.

—*Elizabeth Barrett Browning*

By words the mind is winged.

—*Aristophanes*

Wise men talk because they have something to say; fools talk because they have to say something.

—*Saul Bellow*

A little learning is a dangerous thing / Drink deep, or taste not the Pierian spring.

—*Alexander Pope*

Be not a slave of words.

—*Thomas Carlyle*

The confidence of ignorance will always overcome indecision
of knowledge.

—*Anonymous*

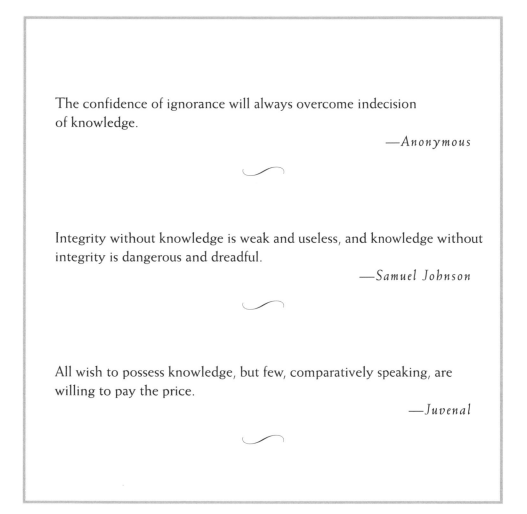

Integrity without knowledge is weak and useless, and knowledge without
integrity is dangerous and dreadful.

—*Samuel Johnson*

All wish to possess knowledge, but few, comparatively speaking, are
willing to pay the price.

—*Juvenal*

True wisdom is less presuming than folly. The wise man doubteth often, and changeth his mind; the fool is obstinate, and doubteth not; he knoweth all things but his own ignorance.

—*Akhenaton*

What really knocks me out is a book that, when you're all done reading it, you wish the author that wrote it was a terrific friend of yours and you could call him up on the phone whenever you felt like it. That doesn't happen much, though.

—*J. D. Salinger*

The art of a people is a true mirror to their minds.

—*Jawaharlal Nehru*

Genius may have its limitations, but stupidity is not thus handicapped.

—*L. Ron Hubbard*

He that studieth revenge keepeth his own wounds green, which otherwise would heal and do well.

—*John Milton*

The first man to use abusive language instead of his fists was the founder of civilization.

—*Sigmund Freud*

Beware the man of a single book.

—*Bertrand Russell*

It requires wisdom to understand wisdom; the music is nothing if the audience is deaf.

—*Walter Lippman*

Happy the man who has broken the chains which hurt the mind, and has given up worrying, once and for all.

—*Ovid*

Human history becomes more and more a race between education and catastrophe.

—H. G. Wells

Genius ain't anything more than elegant common sense.

—Josh Billings

To act with common sense, according to the moment, is the best wisdom I know and the best philosophy is to do one's duties, take the world as it comes, submit respectfully to one's lot; bless the goodness that has given us so much happiness with it, whatever it is; and despise affectation

—Horace Walpole

If you make people think they're thinking, they'll love you; but if you really make them think, they'll hate you.

—*Donald Robert Perry Marquis*

He who asks is a fool for five minutes, but he who does not ask remains a fool forever.

—*Chinese proverb*

A good listener is not only popular everywhere, but after a while he gets to know something.

—*Wilson Mizner*

Education makes a people easy to lead, but difficult to drive; easy to govern but impossible to enslave.

—*Lord Henry Brougham*

A correct answer is like an affectionate kiss.

—*Johann Wolfgang von Goethe*

Wisdom is not a product of schooling but of the lifelong attempt to acquire it.

—*Albert Einstein*

A teacher affects eternity; he can never tell, where his influence stops.

—*Henry Adams*

To teach is to learn twice.

—*Joseph Joubert*

Do not quench your inspiration and your imagination; do not become the slave of your model.

—*Vincent van Gogh*

Style can make complicated things seem simple, or simple things complicated.

—*Jean Cocteau*

Fashions change, but style is forever.

—*Anonymous*

We should be careful to get out of an experience only the wisdom that is in it—and stop there; lest we be like the cat that sits down on a hot stove-lid. She will never sit down on a hot stove-lid again—and that is well; but also she will never sit down on a cold one anymore.

—*Mark Twain*

Truth in science can be defined as the working hypothesis best suited to open the way to the next better one.

—*Konrad Lorenz*

The conventional view serves to protect us from the painful job of thinking.

—*John Kenneth Galbraith*

A man thinks that by mouthing hard words he understands hard things.

—*Herman Melville*

The mind is its own place, and in itself, can make heaven of Hell, and a hell of Heaven.

—*John Milton*

I quote others only in order the better to express myself.

—*Michel de Montaigne*

It is better to be high-spirited even though one makes more mistakes, than to be narrow-minded and too prudent.

—Vincent van Gogh

Poetry begins in delight and ends in wisdom.

—Robert Frost

There is no squabbling so violent as that between people who accepted an idea yesterday and those who will accept the same idea tomorrow.

—Christopher Darlington Morley

A great memory is never made synonymous with wisdom, any more than a dictionary would be called a treatise.

—*John Henry Newman*

Wisdom is ofttimes nearer when we stoop / Than when we soar.

—*William Wordsworth*

True wit is nature to advantage dressed, / What oft was thought, but ne'er so well expressed.

—*Alexander Pope*

It is a good thing for an uneducated man to read books of quotations. Bartlett's Familiar Quotations is an admirable work, and I studied it intently. The quotations when engraved upon the memory give you good thoughts. They also make you anxious to read the authors and look for more.

—*Sir Winston Churchill*

Almost every wise saying has an opposite one, no less wise, to balance it.

—*George Santayana*

Absurdity, n.: A statement or belief manifestly inconsistent with one's own opinion.

—*Ambrose Bierce*

The fool wonders, the wise man asks.

—Benjamin Disraeli

Complaint always comes back in an echo from the ends of the world; but silence strengthens us.

—G. K. Chesterton

There lives more faith in honest doubt, believe me, than in half the creeds.

—Alfred, Lord Tennyson

The ultimate result of shielding men from the effects of folly, is to fill the world with fools.

—*Herbert Spencer*

The liar's punishment is not in the least that he is not believed, but that he cannot believe anyone else.

—*George Bernard Shaw*

Contradiction is not a sign of falsity, nor the lack of contradiction a sign of truth.

—*Blaise Pascal*

To be positive: To be mistaken at the top of one's voice.

—*Ambrose Bierce*

I do not agree with what you say, but I will defend to the death your right to say it.

—*Voltaire*

I never know whether to pity or congratulate a man on coming to his senses.

—*William Makepeace Thackeray*

Some books are undeservedly forgotten; none are undeservedly remembered.

—*W. H. Auden*

True words are not always pretty; pretty words are not always true.

—*Anonymous*

Truth lies within a little and certain compass, but error is immense.

—*Henry St. John*

Never chase a lie. Let it alone, and it will run itself to death.

—*Lyman Beecher*

A man may learn wisdom even from a foe.

—*Aristophenes*

Nobody can be so amusingly arrogant as a young man who has just discovered an old idea and thinks it is his own.

—*Sydney Harris*

The opposite of a correct statement is a false statement. The opposite of a profound truth may well be another profound truth.

—*Niels Bohr*

A belief is not true because it is useful.

—*Henri Frédéric Amiel*

As scarce as truth is, the supply has always been in excess of the demand.

—*Josh Billings*

I do not believe today everything I believed yesterday; I wonder will I believe tomorrow everything I believe today.

—*Matthew Arnold*

A belief is not merely an idea the mind possesses; it is an idea that possesses the mind.

—*Robert Oxton Bolt*

God is in the details.

—*Ludwig Mies van der Rohe*

When a man you like switches from what he said a year ago, or four years ago, he is a broad-minded person who has courage enough to change his mind with changing conditions. When a man you don't like does it, he is a liar who has broken his promises.

—*Franklin P. Adams*

A lie gets halfway around the world before the truth has a chance to get its pants on.

—*Sir Winston Churchill*

Human reason is like a drunken man on horseback; set it up on one side and it tumbles over on the other.

—*Martin Luther*

I passionately hate the idea of being with it, I think an artist has always to be out of step with his time.

—*Orson Welles*

Any great work of art revives and readapts time and space, and the measure of its success is the extent to which it makes you an inhabitant of that world—the extent to which it invites you in and lets you breathe its strange, special air.

—*Leonard Bernstein*

Those who dream by night in the dusty recesses of their minds wake in the day to find that all was vanity, but the dreamers of the day are dangerous men for they may act their dream with open eyes and make it possible.

—*T. E. Lawrence*

Truth that's told with bad intent / Beats all the Lies you can invent.

—*William Blake*

⌒

Keep me away from the wisdom which does not cry, the philosophy which does not laugh, and the greatness which does not bow before children.

—*Kahlil Gibran*

⌒

Man's mind, once stretched by a new idea, never regains its original dimensions.

—*Oliver Wendell Holmes, Jr.*

⌒

Don't talk unless you can improve the silence.

—*Jorge Luis Borges*

The wastebasket is the writer's best friend.

—*Isaac Bashevis Singer*

Where is the wisdom we have lost in knowledge? Where is the knowledge we have lost in information?

—*T. S. Eliot*

Those who will not reason are bigots, those who cannot are fools, and those who dare not are slaves.

—*George Gordon, Lord Byron*

The power of accurate observation is commonly called cynicism by those who have not got it.

—*George Bernard Shaw*

To the artist there is never anything ugly in nature.

—*Auguste Rodin*

Even in the desolate wilderness, stars can still shine.

—*Aoi Jiyuu Shiroi Nozomi*

Peace is not a relationship of nations. It is a condition of mind brought about by a serenity of soul. Peace is not merely the absence of war. It is also a state of mind. Lasting peace can come only to peaceful people.

—*Jawaharlal Nehru*

The sage wears rough clothing and holds the jewel in his heart.

—*Lao-Tzu*

Heard melodies are sweet, but those unheard / Are sweeter . . .

—*John Keats*

Do not the most moving moments of our lives find us all without words?

—*Marcel Marceau*

It is only by introducing the young to great literature, drama and music, and to the excitement of great science that we open to them the possibilities that lie within the human spirit—enable them to see visions and dream dreams.

—*Eric Anderson*

V.

POLITICS
AND
POLITICIANS,
GOVERNMENT
AND
STATESMEN

We the People of the United States, in order to form a more perfect union, establish justice, insure domestic tranquility, provide for the common defense, promote the general welfare, and secure the blessings of liberty to ourselves and our posterity, do ordain and establish this Constitution for the United States of America.

—*Preamble to the Constitution of the United States of America*

We hold these Truths to be self-evident, that all Men are created equal, that they are endowed by their Creator with certain unalienable Rights, that among these are Life, Liberty and the Pursuit of Happiness . . .

—*Declaration of Independence*

I have sworn upon the altar of God, eternal hostility against every form of tyranny over the mind of man.

—*Thomas Jefferson*

All the great things are simple, and many can be expressed in a single word: freedom; justice; honor; duty; mercy; hope.

—Sir Winston Churchill

A nation which makes the final sacrifice for life and freedom does not get beaten.

—Kemal Atatürk

Only our individual faith in freedom can keep us free.

—Dwight D. Eisenhower

Is life so dear, or peace so sweet, as to be purchased at the price of chains and slavery? Forbid it, Almighty God! I know not what course others may take; but as for me, give me liberty or give me death!

—*Patrick Henry*

Those who expect to reap the blessings of freedom must, like men, undergo the fatigue of supporting it.

—*Thomas Paine*

Power tends to corrupt, and absolute power corrupts absolutely.

—*Lord Acton*

Good order is the foundation of all things.

—*Edmund Burke*

Give me the liberty to know, to utter, and to argue freely according to my conscience, above all liberties.

—*John Milton*

All politics is local.

—*Thomas P. "Tip" O'Neil*

They that can give up essential liberty to obtain a little temporary safety deserve neither liberty nor safety.

—*Benjamin Franklin*

If you once forfeit the confidence of your fellow citizens, you can never regain their respect and esteem. You may fool all of the people some of the time; you can even fool some of the people all the time; but you can't fool all of the people all of the time.

—*Abraham Lincoln*

The language of the law must not be foreign to the ears of those who are to obey it.

—*Learned Hand*

The conquer'd, also, and enslaved by war, Shall, with their freedom lost, all virtue lose.

—John Milton

Politics is the art of looking for trouble, finding it whether it exists or not, diagnosing it incorrectly, and applying the wrong remedy.

—Ernest Benn

The hardest thing about any political campaign is how to win without proving that you are unworthy of winning.

—Theodor Adorno

A society of sheep must in time beget a government of wolves.

—*Bertrand de Jouvenel*

Freedom is like drink. If you take any at all, you might as well take enough to make you happy for a while.

—*Finley Peter Dunne*

If liberty means anything at all, it means the right to tell people what they do not want to hear.

—*George Orwell*

If we do not believe in freedom of speech for those we despise we do not believe in it at all.

—*Noam Chomsky*

Most people do not really want freedom, because freedom involves responsibility, and most people are frightened of responsibility.

—*Sigmund Freud*

You can only protect your liberties in this world by protecting the other man's freedom. You can only be free if I am free.

—*Clarence Darrow*

The measure of a man is what he does with power.

—*Pittacus*

All that is necessary for the triumph of evil is that good men do nothing.

—*Edmund Burke*

A single death is a tragedy; a million deaths is a statistic.

—*Joseph Stalin*

Mankind is at its best when it is most free. This will be clear if we grasp the principle of liberty. We must recall that the basic principle of liberty is freedom of choice, which saying many have on their lips but few in their minds.

—*Dante Alighieri*

The buck stops here.

—*Harry S. Truman*

The first method for estimating the intelligence of a ruler is to look at the men he has around him.

—*Niccolò Machiavelli*

The language of the law must not be foreign to the ear of those who are to obey it.

—*Learned Hand*

Being powerful is like being a lady. If you have to tell people you are—you aren't.

—*Margaret Thatcher*

A leader or a man of action in a crisis almost always acts subconsciously and then thinks of the reasons for his action.

—*Jawaharlal Nehru*

Who controls the past controls the future. Who controls the present controls the past.

—*George Orwell*

It is better to die on your feet than to live on your knees.

—*Emiliano Zapata*

You can discover what your enemy fears most by observing the means he uses to frighten you.

—*Eric Hoffer*

The very essence of a free government consists in considering offices as public trusts, bestowed for the good of the country, and not for the benefit of an individual or a party.

—*John C. Calhoun*

The free, exploring mind of the individual human is the most valuable thing in the world. And this I would fight for: the freedom of the mind to take any direction it wishes, undirected. And this I must fight against: any idea, religion, or government which limits or destroys the individual.

—*John Steinbeck*

Justice delayed is justice denied.

—*Legal maxim*

I only ask to be free. The butterflies are free.

—*Charles Dickens*

The true greatness of nations is in those qualities which constitute the greatness of the individual.

—*Charles Sumner*

The best use of laws is to teach men to trample bad laws under their feet.

—*Wendell Phillips*

Politics is an inexact science.

—Otto von Bismarck

We hold these truths to be self-evident, that all men and women are created equal.

—Elizabeth Cady Stanton

No taxation without representation.

—Rallying cry of the American Revolution

No man is above the law and no man is below it; nor do we ask any man's permission when we require him to obey it. Obedience of the law is demanded; not asked as a favor.

—*Theodore Roosevelt*

I must study politics and war that my sons may have liberty to study mathematics and philosophy.

—*John Adams*

A people that values its privileges above its principles soon loses both.

—*Dwight D. Eisenhower*

The right to be heard does not automatically include the right to be taken seriously.

—*Hubert H. Humphrey*

The death of democracy is not likely to be an assassination from ambush. It will be a slow extinction from apathy, indifference, and undernourishment.

—*Robert Hutchins*

The man who strikes first admits that his ideas have given out.

—*Chinese proverb*

It is inaccurate to say I hate everything. I am strongly in favor of common sense, common honesty, and common decency. This makes me forever ineligible for any public office.

—*H. L. Mencken*

Freedom of thought and the right to private judgment, in matters of conscience, driven from every corner of the earth, direct their course to this happy country as their last asylum. Let us cherish the noble guests, and shelter them under the wings of universal toleration.

—*Samuel Adams*

There are few things wholly evil or wholly good. Almost everything, especially of government policy, is an inseparable compound of the two, so that our best judgment of the preponderance between them is continually demanded.

—*Abraham Lincoln*

Those who corrupt the public mind are just as evil as those who steal from the public purse.

—*Adlai E. Stevenson*

A man's feet should be planted in his country, but his eyes should survey the world.

—*George Santayana*

In politics stupidity is not a handicap.

—*Napoléon Bonaparte*

Nothing in life is certain except death and taxes.

—*Benjamin Franklin*

I expose slavery in this country, because to expose it is to kill it. Slavery is one of those monsters of darkness to whom the light of truth is death.

—*Frederick Douglass*

The true republic: men, their rights and nothing more; women, their rights and nothing less.

—*Franklin P. Adams*

I know not with what weapons World War III will be fought, but World War IV will be fought with sticks and stones.

—*Albert Einstein*

Practical politics consists in ignoring facts.

—*Henry Brooks Adams*

Even when laws have been written down, they ought not always to remain unaltered.

—*Aristotle*

Toleration is good for all, or it is good for none.

—*Edmund Burke*

The whole history of the progress of human liberty shows that all concessions yet made to her august claims have been born of earnest struggle. . . . If there is no struggle, there is no progress. Those who profess to favor freedom, and yet deprecate agitation, are men who want crops without plowing up the ground, they want rain without thunder and lightning. They want the ocean without the awful roar of its many waters.

—*Frederick Douglass*

In the country of the blind the one-eyed man is king.

—*Deciderius Erasmus*

The Law, in its majestic equality, forbids the rich, as well as the poor, to sleep under the bridges, to beg in the streets, and to steal bread.

—*Anatole France*

Cautious, careful people always casting about to preserve their reputation or social standards never can bring about reform. Those who are really in earnest are willing to be anything or nothing in the world's estimation, and publicly and privately, in season and out, avow their sympathies with despised ideas and their advocates, and bear the consequences.

—*Susan B. Anthony*

One man with courage is a majority.

—*Thomas Jefferson*

Injustice anywhere is a threat to justice everywhere.

—*Martin Luther King, Jr.*

Let the word go forth from this time and place, to friend and foe alike, that the torch has been passed to a new generation of Americans—born in this century, tempered by war, disciplined by a hard and bitter peace, proud of our ancient heritage—and unwilling to witness or permit the slow undoing of those human rights to which this Nation has always been committed, and to which we are committed today at home and around the world.

Let every nation know, whether it wishes us well or ill, that we shall pay any price, bear any burden, meet any hardship, support any friend, oppose any foe, in order to assure the survival and the success of liberty.

So let us begin anew—remembering on both sides that civility is not a sign of weakness, and sincerity is always subject to proof. Let us never negotiate out of fear. But let us never fear to negotiate.

All this will not be finished in the first 100 days. Nor will it be finished in the first 1,000 days, nor in the life of this Administration, nor even perhaps in our lifetime on this planet. But let us begin.

And so, my fellow Americans: ask not what your country can do for you—ask what you can do for your country.

—*John F. Kennedy*

If mankind minus one were of one opinion, then mankind is no more justified in silencing the one than the one—if he had the power—would be justified in silencing mankind.

—*John Stuart Mill*

The politician is . . . trained in the art of inexactitude. His words tend to be blunt or rounded, because if they have a cutting edge they may later return to wound him.

—*Edward R. Murrow*

Bad officials are elected by good citizens who do not vote.

—*George Jean Nathan*

War is delightful to those who have had no experience of it.
—*Desiderius Erasmus*

You cannot simultaneously prevent and prepare for war.
—*Albert Einstein*

Man's capacity for justice makes democracy possible; but man's inclination to injustice makes democracy necessary.
—*Reinhold Niebuhr*

The nine most terrifying words in the English language are, "I'm from the government and I'm here to help."

—*Ronald Reagan*

Laws do not persuade just because they threaten.

—*Seneca*

If you can't stand the heat, get out of the kitchen.

—*Harry S. Truman*

Politicians are the same all over. They promise to build bridges even when there are no rivers.

—*Nikita Khruschev*

One cool judgment is worth a dozen hasty councils. The thing to do is to supply light and not heat.

—*Woodrow Wilson*

Rebellion to tyrants is obedience to God.

—*Thomas Jefferson*

If the misery of the poor be caused not by the laws of nature, but by our institutions, great is our sin.

—*Charles Darwin*

Law is order, and good law is good order.

—*Aristotle*

Man is born free; and everywhere he is in chains. One thinks himself the master of others, and still remains a greater slave than they. How did this change come about? I do not know. What can make it legitimate? That question I think I can answer. If I took into account only force, and the effects derived from it, I should say: As long as a people is compelled to obey, and obeys, it does well; as soon as it can shake off the yoke, and shakes it off, it does still better; for, regaining its liberty by the same right as took it away, either it is justified in resuming it, or there was no justification for those who took it away. But the social order is a sacred right which is the basis of all other rights. Nevertheless, this right does not come from nature, and must therefore be founded on conventions.

—*Jean-Jacques Rousseau*

Liberty is the right to silence.
> —*Graffiti during French student riots, 1968*

In some cases non-violence requires more militancy than violence.
> —*César Chávez*

In the province of the mind, what one believes to be true either is true or becomes true.
> —*John Lilly*

Freedom . . . is not ours by inheritance; it must be fought for and defended constantly by each generation, for it comes only once to a people. Those who have known freedom, and then lost it, have never known it again.

—*Ronald Reagan*

The future days, which we seek to make secure, we look forward to a world founded upon four essential human freedoms. The first is freedom of speech and expression—everywhere in the world. The second is freedom of every person to worship God in his own way—everywhere in the world. The third is freedom from want—which, translated into world terms, means economic understandings which will secure to every nation a healthy peacetime life for its inhabitants—everywhere in the world. The fourth is freedom from fear—which, translated into world terms, means a world-wide reduction of armaments to such a point and in such a thorough fashion that no nation will be in a position to commit an act of physical aggression against any neighbor—anywhere in the world.

—*Franklin Delano Roosevelt*

Of all times in time of war the press should be free.

—*William Borah*

The greatest dangers to liberty lurk in insidious encroachment by men of zeal, well-meaning, but without understanding.

—*Louis D. Brandeis*

You have not converted a man because you have silenced him.

—*Viscount John Morley*

I know war as few men now living know it, and nothing to me is more revolting. I have long advocated its complete abolition, as its very destructiveness on both friend and foe has rendered it useless as a means of settling international disputes.

—*General Douglas MacArthur*

If a nation values anything more than freedom, it will lose its freedom; and the irony of it is that if it is comfort or money that it values more, it will lose that too.

—*W. Somerset Maugham*

Freedom is not worth having if it does not connote freedom to err. It passes my comprehension how human beings, be they ever so experienced and able, can delight in depriving other human beings of that precious right.

—*Mohandas Gandhi*

The punishment which the wise suffer who refuse to take part in the government, is to live under the government of worse men.

—Plato

To give up the task of reforming society is to give up one's responsibility as a free man.

—Alan Paton

We learn from history that we do not learn from history.

—Georg Wilhelm Friedrich Hegel

Man does not live by words alone, despite the fact that sometimes he has to eat them.

—*Adlai E. Stevenson*

The most effective way of attacking vice is to expose it to public ridicule. People can put up with rebukes, but they cannot bear being laughed at: they are prepared to be wicked but they dislike appearing ridiculous.

—*Molière*

Freedom is man's capacity to take a hand in his own development. It is our capacity to mold ourselves.

—*Rollo May*

When people are free to do as they please, they usually imitate each other

—*Eric Hoffer*

The united voice of millions cannot lend the smallest foundation to falsehood.

—*Oliver Goldsmith*

When you are right, you cannot be too radical; When you are wrong, you cannot be too conservative.

—*Martin Luther King, Jr.*

Heresy is another word for freedom of thought.

—*Graham Greene*

A government that is big enough to give you all you want is big enough to take it all away.

—*Barry Goldwater*

Men are not hanged for stealing horses, but that horses may not be stolen.

—*George Savile, Marquess of Halifax*

The basis of our political system is the right of the people to make and to alter their constitutions of government.

—*George Washington*

Freedom of the mind requires not only, or not even specially, the absence of legal constraints but the presence of alternative thoughts. The most successful tyranny is not the one that uses force to assure uniformity but the one that removes the awareness of other possibilities.

—*Alan Bloom*

The hottest places in hell are reserved for those who in times of great moral crises maintain their neutrality.

—*Dante Alighieri*

America will never be destroyed from the outside. If we falter and lose our freedoms, it will be because we destroyed ourselves.

—*Abraham Lincoln*

No one flower can ever symbolize this nation. America is a bouquet.

—*William Safire*

VI

PROVERBIAL WISDOM

A country can be judged by the quality of its proverbs.

—German proverb

A handful of patience is worth more than a bushel of brains.

—Dutch proverb

It is easy to despise what you cannot get.

—Aesop, "The Fox and the Grapes"
(the origin of the phrase "sour grapes")

A quiet fool is half a sage.

—Yiddish proverb

A bird in the hand is worth two in the bush.

—English proverb

It is thrifty to prepare today for the wants of tomorrow.
—Aesop, "The Ant and the Grasshopper"

Union gives strength.

—Aesop, "The Bundle of Sticks"

If you want to give God a good laugh, tell Him your plans.

—Yiddish proverb

Please all, and you will please none.

—Aesop, "The Man, the Boy, and the Donkey"

Since the house is on fire, let us warm ourselves.

—Italian proverb

People often grudge others what they cannot enjoy themselves.

—Aesop, "The Dog in the Manger"

We often give our enemies the means of our own destruction.

—Aesop, "The Eagle and the Arrow"

It is easy to be brave from a safe distance.

—Aesop, "The Wolf and the Kid"

Don't think there are no crocodiles because the water is calm.

—Malayan proverb

Do not count your chickens before they are hatched.

—Aesop, "The Milk Woman and Her Pail"

A journey of a thousand miles begins with a single step.

—Chinese proverb

An army of sheep led by a lion would defeat an army of lions led by a sheep.

—Arab proverb

Procrastination is the thief of time.

—Proverb found in many cultures

Beware lest you lose the substance by grasping at the shadow.
—*Aesop, "The Dog and the Shadow"*

Luck is like having a rice dumpling fly into your mouth.
—*Japanese proverb*

The best armor is to keep out of range.
—*Italian proverb*

Men often applaud an imitation, and hiss the real thing.
—*Aesop, "The Buffoon and the Countryman"*

Better to light a candle than to curse the darkness.
—*Chinese proverb*

When spiders unite, they can tie down a lion.
—*Ethiopian proverb*

Love is friendship set on fire.

—French proverb

The death of a friend is equivalent to the loss of a limb.

—German proverb

Dance as if no one's watching, sing as if no one's listening, and live everyday as if it were your last.

—Irish proverb

The reverse side also has a reverse side.

—Japanese proverb

At the end of the game, the king and the pawn go back in the same box.

—Italian proverb

The older the fiddle, the sweeter the tune.

—Irish proverb

Vision without action is daydream. Action without vision is nightmare.

—Japanese proverb

The generous and bold have the best lives.

—Norwegian proverb

Fear is only as deep as the mind allows.

—Japanese proverb

Turn your face to the sun and the shadows fall behind you.

—Maori proverb

To be damned by the devil is to be truly blessed.

—*Chinese proverb*

It is better to live one day as a lion, than a thousand days as a lamb.

—*Roman proverb*

The church is close, but the road is icey. The tavern is far, but I will walk carefully.

—*Russian proverb*

Water that does not move, is always shallow.

—Sami proverb

He who allows his day to pass by without practicing generosity and enjoying life's pleasures is like a blacksmith's bellows—he breathes but does not live.

—Sanskrit proverb

Be humble for you are made of earth. Be noble for you are made of stars.

—Serbian proverb

It takes an entire village to raise a child

—African proverb

Fear less, hope more; eat less, chew more; whine less, breathe more; talk less, say more; hate less, love more; and all good things are yours.

—Swedish proverb

Slow and steady wins the race.

—Aesop, "The Tortoise and the Hare"

By asking for the impossible, obtain the best possible.

—Italian proverb

Call on God, but row away from the rocks.

—Indian proverb

If you must play, decide on three things at the start: the rules of the game, the stakes, and the quitting time.

—Chinese proverb

Even a clock that does not work is right twice a day.

—*Polish proverb*

He who hurries can not walk with dignity.

—*Chinese proverb*

Don't throw away the old bucket until you know whether the new one holds water.

—*Swedish proverb*

It's the final straw that broke the camel's back.

—*English proverb*

Tell me and I'll forget. Show me, and I may not remember. Involve me, and I'll understand.

—*Native American proverb*

What's good for the goose is good for the gander.

—*English proverb*

He who lies down with dogs, rises with fleas.

—*English proverb*

A man is not honest simply because he never had a chance to steal.

—*Russian proverb*

The innkeeper loves the drunkard, but not for a son-in-law.

—*Yiddish proverb*

Time and words can't be recalled, even if it was only yesterday.

—*Estonian proverb*

You won't help shoots grow by pulling them up higher.

—*Chinese proverb*

Cursing the weather is never good farming.

—*English proverb*

Too many cooks spoil the broth.

—*English proverb*

Ask the experienced rather than the learned.

—*Arabic proverb*

Waste not, want not.

—*Proverb found in many cultures*

Tomorrow is often the busiest time of the year.

—*Spanish proverb*

When I rest, I rust.

—*German proverb*

Revenge is a dish best served cold.

—*Italian proverb*

He who is outside his door has the hardest part of his journey
behind him.

—*Flemish proverb*

Nobody's sweetheart is ugly.

—*Dutch proverb*

The wagon rests in winter, the sleigh in summer, the horse never.

—*Yiddish proverb*

Birds of a feather flock together.

—*English proverb*

Lend a horse, and you may have back his skin.

—English proverb

You can't hatch chickens from fried eggs.

—German proverb

Care, and not fine stables, makes a good horse.

—Danish proverb

Trees often transplanted seldom prosper.

—Flemish proverb

Roasted pigeons will not fly into one's mouth.

—Dutch proverb

The early bird catches the worm.

—English proverb

One meets his destiny often in the road he takes to avoid it.

—*French proverb*

When the cat's away, the mice will play.

—*French proverb*

All cats appear grey in the dark.

—*English proverb*

Curiosity killed the cat.

—English proverb

You can't dance at two weddings at the same time; nor can you sit on two horses with one behind.

—Yiddish proverb

When rats infest the palace, a lame cat is better than the swiftest horse.

—Chinese proverb

Let sleeping dogs lie.

—French proverb

There are plenty more fish in the sea.

—English proverb

Whoever gossips to you will gossip about you.

—Spanish proverb

Don't change horses in the middle of the stream.

—Dutch proverb

You can lead a horse to water, but you can't make him drink.

—English proverb

It's too late to close the stable door after the horse has bolted.

—French proverb

Even the candle seller dies in the dark.

—Colombian proverb

A road to a friend's house is never long.

—Danish proverb

Speak silver, reply gold.

—Swahili proverb

When two elephants fight it is the grass that suffers.

—African proverb

He who does nothing makes no mistakes.

—Italian proverb

When one door shuts, a hundred open.

—Spanish proverb

The greedy man stores all but friendship.

—Irish proverb

If a little money does not go out, great money will not come in.

—*Chinese proverb*

A people without history is like the wind on the buffalo grass.

—*Lakota Sioux proverb*

Joy shared is twice the joy. Sorrow shared is half the sorrow.

—*Swedish proverb*

Least said, soonest mended.

—*Irish proverb*

A rich child often sits in a poor mother's lap.

—*Danish proverb*

A fool and his money are soon parted.

—*English proverb*

Worry gives a small thing a big shadow.

—*Swedish proverb*

The gods help them that help themselves.

—*Aesop, "Hercules and the Waggoner"*

Sparrows that emulate peacocks are likely to break a thigh.

—*Burmese proverb*

Do not judge a man until you have walked two moons in his moccasins.

—*Native American proverb*

However long the night, the dawn will break.

—*African proverb*

Appearances often are deceiving.

—*Aesop, "The Wolf and the Lamb"*

Big mouthfuls often choke.

—*Italian proverb*

Familiarity breeds contempt.

—Aesop, "The Fox and the Lion"

Pride goeth before destruction, and haughty spirit before a fall.

—The Bible, Proverbs 16:18

If you want people to think you are wise, agree with them.

—Yiddish proverb

Blessed is the man who can laugh at himself, for he will never cease to be amused.

—Proverb found in many cultures

Selected Quoted Sources

Abdul-Jabar, Kareem (b. 1947), American basketball player
Abert, Geoffrey F., Late-twentieth-century American author
Acheson, Dean (1893–1971), U.S. secretary of state
Acton, Lord (John Dalberg-Acton) (1834–1902), English historian
Adams, Abigail (1744–1818), American writer and first lady
Adams, Franklin P. (1881–1960), American columnist and author
Adams, George Matthew, Early-twentieth-century novelist
Adams, Henry Brooks (1838–1918), American historian and writer
Adams, John (1735–1826), Second U.S. president
Adams, Samuel (1722–1803), American Revolutionary patriot
Adams, Scott (b. 1957), American cartoonist and creator of "Dilbert"
Addison, Joseph (1672–1719), English essayist, poet, statesman
Adler, Stella (1901–1992), American stage actress
Adorno, Theodor (1903–1969), German philosopher and sociologist
Aeschylus (525–456 B.C.), Greek tragic dramatist
Aesop (c. 500 B.C.–?), Greek fabulist
Akhenaton (d. c. 1354 B.C.), Egyptian king

Alcott, Bronson (1799–1888), American educational and social reformer

Alcott, Louisa May (1832–1888), American novelist

Algren, Nelson (1909–1981), American novelist

Ali, Muhammad (b.1942), American boxer

Alighieri, Dante (1265–1321), Italian poet

Allen, Woody (b. 1935), American comedian, actor, and producer

Amiel, Henri Frédéric (1821–1881), Swiss philosopher and poet

Angelou, Maya, (b. 1928), American author, poet laureate, and composer

Anouilh, Jean (1910–1987), French playwright

Anthony, Susan B. (1820–1906), American leader of the women's suffrage movement

Archimedes (287 B.C.–212 B.C.), Greek physicist and mathematician

Aristophanes (c. 448 B.C.–c. 388 B.C.), Athenian playwright

Aristotle (384 B.C.–322 B.C.), Greek philosopher

Arnold, Matthew (1822–1888), British poet and critic

Asimov, Isaac (1920–1992), Russian-American science-fiction writer and scientist

Assisi, Saint Francis of (1182–1226), Founder of the Franciscan order

Astaire, Fred (1899–1987), American dancer and actor

Astor, Lady Nancy (1879–1964), English politician

Atatürk, Kemal (1881–1938), Turkish soldier and founder of modern Turkey

Athenaeus, Second-century Greek grammarian and rhetorician

Auden, W(ystan) H(ugh) (1907–1973), British-American writer and critic

Augustine, Saint (354 A.D.–430 A.D.), Early Christian theologian and bishop

Aurelius, Marcus (121 A.D. –180 A.D.), Roman emperor

Austen, Jane (1775–1817), British writer

Bach, Richard (b. 1936), American writer

Bacon, Francis (1909–1992), Irish artist

Bacon, Sir Francis (1561–1626), philosopher and essayist

Baez, Joan (b. 1941), American folk singer and political activist

Bagehot, Walter (1826–1877), British journalist and economist

Bailey, Pearl (1918–1990), American singer and actress

Baldwin, James (1924–1987), American critic and writer
Ball, Lucille, (1911–1989), American actress and comedienne
Balzac, Honoré de (1799–1850), French writer
Bannister, Roger (b. 1929), British long-distance runner
Barrie, Sir James Matthew (1860–1937), British writer
Barton, Bruce (1886–1967), American congressman
Baruch, Bernard Mannes (1870–1965), American political advisor and stockbroker
Barzun, Jacques Martin (b.1907), American educator
Beecher, Lyman (1775–1863), American Presbyterian clergyman
Beethoven, Ludwig van (1770–1827), German composer
Behan, Brendan Francis (1923–1964), Irish dramatist
Bellow, Saul (b.1915), American novelist
Benn, Ernest (1875–?), English publisher
Bennett, Arnold (Enoch) (1867–1931), British novelist
Bennett, William John (b. 1943), U.S. secretary of education
Bennis, Warren G. (b. 1925), American educator and sociologist
Bernstein, Leonard (1918–1990), American composer
Berra, Laurence "Yogi" (b. 1925), American baseball player
Besant, Sir Walter (1836–1901), English novelist and humanitarian
Bierce, Ambrose (1842–1914), American journalist
Billings, Josh (1818–1885), American humorous essayist
Blake, Eubie (1883–1983), American ragtime pianist and composer
Blake, William (1757–1827), British poet
Bloom, Alan (1930–1992), American sociologist and writer
Bohr, Niels (1885–1962), Danish physicist
Boileau, Nicolas (1636–1711), French literary critic and poet
Bolt, Robert Oxton (b. 1924), English author
Bombeck, Erma (Louise) (b.1927), American author
Bonaparte, Napoléon (1769–1821), French general
Boorstin, Daniel J. (b. 1914), U.S. librarian of Congress

Borah, William (1865–1940), U.S. senator
Borge, Victor (1909–2000), Danish-American pianist and comedian
Borges, Jorge Luis (1899–1986), Argentinian writer
Bowen, Catherine Drinker (1897–1973), American writer
Bradbury, Ray (b. 1920), American science-fiction writer
Brandeis, Louis D. (1856–1941), U.S. Supreme Court justice
Braque, Georges (1882–1963), French painter
Brontë, Charlotte (1816–1855), British novelist
Brothers, Dr. Joyce (b. 1929), American psychologist
Brougham, Lord Henry (1778–1868), British statesman
Brown, James (b.1933), American soul singer
Browning, Elizabeth Barrett (1806–1861), British poet
Browning, Robert (1812–1889), British poet
Bryan, William Jennings (1860–1925), American lawyer and politician
Bryant, William Cullen (1794–1878), American poet and newspaper editor
Buck, Pearl (1892–1973), American missionary and writer
Buddha, Siddhártha Gautama (c. 563 B.C.–c. 483 B.C.), founder of Buddhism
Bukowski, Charles (1920–1994), German-American poet and novelist
Bulwer-Lytton, Edward George (1803–1873), British novelist and poet
Burke, Edmund (1729–1797), British political writer and statesman
Burnett, Leo, Twentieth-century advertising executive
Burns, Robert (1759–1796), Scottish poet
Buscaglia, Leo (b.1924), American educator
Bush, Barbara (b.1925), American first lady
Butler, Samuel (1612–1680), English poet and author
Byrnes, James F. (1879–1972), U.S. secretary of state
Byron, George Gordon, Lord (1788–1824), English romantic poet
Campbell, Joseph (1904–1987), American mythologist
Camus, Albert (1913–1960), French existential philosopher and writer
Capone, Al (1899–1947), Italian-American organized crime boss

Capra, Frank (1897–1991), American film director
Carlyle, Thomas (1795–1881), British historian
Carnegie, Dale (1888–1955), American self-improvement author
Carroll, Lewis (1832–1898), British writer
Carver, George Washington (1864–1943), American agricultural chemist and inventor
Cervantes, Miguel de (1547–1616), Spanish writer
Chaplin, Charlie (1889–1977), English silent-film actor
Chávez, César (1927–1993), American agrarian labor leader
Chesterfield, Philip Dormer Stanhope, Lord (1694–1773), English writer and politician
Chesterton, G. K. (1974–1936), English author
Chomsky, Noam (b. 1928), educator, linguist, and political writer
Christie, Agatha (1890–1976), English mystery writer
Churchill, Sir Winston (1874–1965), English prime minister
Cicero, Marcus Tullius (106 B.C.–43 B.C.), Roman orator
Cocteau, Jean (1891–1963), French avant-garde writer, filmmaker, and artist
Coleridge, Samuel Taylor (1772–1834), English romantic poet
Colton, Charles Caleb (1780–1832), American clergyman and writer
Conan Doyle, Sir Arthur (1859–1930), British author
Confucius (c. 551 B.C.–479 B.C.), Chinese philosopher
Conrad, Joseph (1857–1924), British novelist
Conroy, Pat (b. 1945), American writer
Cooke, Alistair (1908–2004), British-American journalist and radio/TV personality
Coolidge, Calvin (1872–1933), Thirtieth U.S. president
Cosby, Bill (b. 1937), American comedian and actor
Cousins, Norman (1915–1990), American editor and author
Crisp, Quentin (1908–1999), English autobiographer
Crumb, Robert (b. 1943), social and political cartoonist
cummings, e.e. (1894–1962), American author
da Vinci, Leonardo (1492–1519), Italian artist and innovator
Darrow, Clarence (1857–1938), American lawyer

Darwin, Charles (1809–1882), English naturalist and evolutionary theorist
Davies, Robertson (b. 1913), Canadian novelist
Davis, Bette (1908–1989), American film actress
Davis, Jefferson (1808–1889), President of the Confederacy during the Civil War
Davis, Miles Jr. (1926–1991), American jazz musician
de Buffon, George-Louis (1707–1788), French naturalist and author
de Bussy-Rabutin, Comte Roger (1618–1693), French satirical writer
de Jouvenel, Bertrand (1903–1987), French writer
de la Rochefoucauld, François (1613–1680), French author
DeMille, Cecil B. (1881–1959), film director and producer
de Montaigne, Michel (1533–1592), French essayist
de Bergerac, Cyrano (1619–1655), large-nosed French writer
Demosthenes (384 B.C.–322 B.C.), Greek orator
Deng Xiaoping (1904–1997), Chinese revolutionary and government leader
Descartes, René (1596–1650), French philosopher and mathemetician
Dewey, John (1859–1952), American philosopher and educator
Dickens, Charles (1812–1870), English novelist
Dickinson, Emily (1830–1836), American poet
Disraeli, Benjamin (1804–1881), British prime minister and author
Donne, John (1572–1631), British metaphysical poet
Dostoyevsky, Fyodor Mikhaylovich (1821–1881), Russian novelist
Douglass, Frederick (1817–1895), American abolitionist, author, and orator
Dryden, John (1631–1700), English poet laureate
Dumas, Alexandre (1802–1870), French author
Dunne, Finley Peter (1867–1936), American humorist
Durant, Will (1885–1981), American historian and essayist
Dylan, Bob (b.1941), American songwriter
Edison, Thomas Alva (1847–1931), American inventor
Einstein, Albert (1879–1955), Austrian-American theoretical physicist
Eisenhower, Dwight David (1890–1969), Thirty-fourth U.S. president

Eliot, George, pseudonym of Mary Ann Evans (1819–1880), English novelist

Eliot, T. S. (1885–1968), British poet and winner of the Nobel Prize for Literature

Ellington, Duke (1899–1974), American jazz musician

Emerson, Ralph Waldo (1803–1882), American philosopher and poet

Epictetus (c. 50 A.D. –c. 138 A.D.), Phrygian Stoic philosopher

Epicurus (341 B.C.–270 B.C.), Greek philosopher

Erasmus, Deciderius (c.1466–1536), Dutch Renaissance theologian

Ertz, Susan (1894–1985), British novelist

Euripides (c. 480 B.C.–406 B.C.), Greek dramatist

Evert, Chris (b. 1954), American tennis player

Fadiman, Clifton (1904–1999), American literary critic

Faulkner, William (1897–1962), American author and Nobel Prize winner

Fenwick, Millicent (1910–1992), American diplomat and congresswoman

Fitzgerald, F. Scott (1896–1940), American novelist

Flagg, Fanny (b. 1944), American author of *Fried Green Tomatoes*

Forbes, Malcolm (1919–1990), American magazine publisher

Ford, Henry (1863–1947), American automobile manufacturer

Forster, E(dward) M(organ) (1879–1970), British author

France, Anatole (1844–1924), French writer and critic

Frank, Anne (1929–1945), Dutch World War II diarist

Franklin, Benjamin (1706–1790), American statesman and writer

Freud, Anna (1895–1982), British psychoanalyst and daughter of Sigmund Freud

Freud, Sigmund (1856–1939), Austrian psychoanalyst

Fromm, Erich (1900–1980), German psychoanalyst and author

Fromme, Allan, Twentieth-century author on relationships

Frost, Robert (1874–1963), American poet

Fuentes, Carlos (b. 1928), Mexican writer and diplomat

Fuller, R. Buckminster (1895–1983), American architect and engineer

Fuller, Thomas (1608–1661), English clergyman and author

Galbraith, John Kenneth (b. 1908), American economist and public official

Galilei, Galileo (1564–1642), Italian astronomer and physicist
Gandhi, Mohandas (1869–1948), Indian nonviolent nationalist
Garcia, Jerry (1942–1995), Singer and songwriter for The Grateful Dead
Geisel, Theodore, See Seuss, Dr.
Gibbon, Edward (1737–1794), British historian
Gibran, Kahlil (1883–1931), Lebanese-American poet and novelist
Gide, André (1869–1951), French writer
Gilbert, Sir William S. (1836–1911), English playwright, librettist, and poet
Goethe, Johann Wolfgang von (1749–1832), German poet, dramatist, and novelist
Goldsmith, Oliver (c. 1730–1774), British-Irish author and dramatist
Goldwater, Barry (1909–1998), U.S. senator
Goya, Francisco de (1746–1828), Spanish painter
Graham, Billy (b. 1918), American Evangelical preacher
Graham, Martha (1894–1991), American modern dancer and choreographer
Greene, Graham (1904–1991), English novelist and playwright
Gretzky, Wayne (b. 1961), Canadian ice-hockey player
Guevara, Ernesto "Che" (1928–1967), Cuban revolutionary leader
Guthrie, Woody (1912–1967), American folk singer and composer
Hagen, Walter (1892–1969), American golfer
Hammarskjöld, Dag (1905–1961), Secretary-general of the United Nations
Hand, Learned (1872–1961), Judge of the Federal Court of Appeals
Harburg, E. Y. (1898–1981), American composer
Harris, Sydney, American cartoonist and author
Hardy, Thomas (1840–1928), English novelist
Harvey, Paul (b. 1918), American radio broadcaster
Hawking, Stephen (b. 1942), British theoretical physicist
Hawthorne, Nathaniel (1804–1864), American writer
Hazlitt, William (1778–1830), British essayist
Hecht, Ben (1894–1964), American writer
Hegel, Georg Wilhelm Friedrich (1770–1831), German philosopher

Hemingway, Ernest (1899–1961), American writer

Henry, Patrick (1736–1799), American statesman

Heraclitus (c. 535 B.C.–c. 475 B.C.), Greek philosopher

Herodotus (c.484–c.425 B.C.), Greek historian

Hesse, Herman (1877–1962), German novelist and poet

Hillel, Rabbi, ancient Babylonian Jewish scholar

Hoffer, Eric (1902–1983), American self-educated longshoreman and author

Holmes, Oliver Wendell Jr. (1841–1935), Supreme Court justice

Holtz, Lou (b. 1937), American college football coach

Homer, Seventh-century B.C. Greek poet

Horace (65 B.C.–8 B.C.), Latin poet

Hoyle, Edmond (1672–1769), British writer

Hubbard, L. Ron (1911–1986), American science-fiction writer

Hughes, Charles Evans (1862–1948), Associate justice of the U.S. Supreme Court

Hugo, Victor (1802–1825), French writer, poet, and dramatist

Hume, David (1711–1776), Scottish philosopher and historian

Humphrey, Hubert H. (1911–1978), U.S. vice president

Hutchins, Robert (1899–1977), American educator

Huxley, Aldous (1894–1963), British novelist

Ibsen, Henrik (1828–1906), Norwegian dramatist and poet

Ingersoll, Robert (1833–1899), American orator and lawyer

Jackson, Andrew (1767–1845), Seventh U.S. president

Jagger, Mick (b. 1943), English lead singer of The Rolling Stones

James, William (1842–1910), American psychologist and philosopher

Jefferson, Thomas (1743–1826), Third U.S. president

John Paul II (b. 1920), Pope

John XXIII (1881–1963), Italian Pope

Johnson, Samuel (1709–1784), English author

Joubert, Joseph (1754–1824), French moralist

Joyce, James (1882–1941), Irish novelist

Jung, Carl (1875–1961), Swiss psychiatrist

Juvenal (c. 60 A.D.–c. 140 A.D.), Roman satirist

Kafka, Franz (1883–1924), Bohemian novelist

Kaiser, Henry J. (1882–1967), American industrialist

Kant, Immanuel (1724–1804), German metaphysical philosopher

Kaye, Danny (1913–1987), American actor, singer, and comedian

Keats, John (1795–1821), English poet

Keller, Helen (1880–1968), American writer and lecturer

Kennedy, John F. (1917–1963), Thirty-fifth U.S. president

Kennedy, Robert Francis (1925–1968), U.S. attorney general

Kenny, Elizabeth (1886–1952), Australian nurse and author

Khayyam, Omar, Eleventh-century Persian poet and mathematician

Khrushchev, Nikita (1894–1971), Soviet Communist premier of the USSR

Kierkegaard, Søren (1813–1855), Danish philosopher

Laërtius, Diogenes, Third-century Greek biographer

Landers, Ann, Twentieth-century American advice columnist

Lao-Tzu, Sixth-century Chinese philosopher

Lawrence, D. H. (1885–1930), British novelist

Lawrence, T. E. (1888–1935), British adventurer and soldier, known as Lawrence of Arabia

Lee, Harper (b. 1926), American Pulitzer Prize-winning novelist

Lemmon, Jack (1925–2001), American actor

Lewis, C. S. (1898–1963), British writer

Lichtenberg, Georg Christoph (1742–1799), German physicist and satirist

Lilly, John (c.1554–1606), English dramatist and prose writer

Lincoln, Abraham (1809–1865), Sixteenth U.S. president

Lippman, Walter J. (1889–1974), American journalist and Pulitzer Prize winner

Locke, John (1632–1704), English empirical philosopher

Lombardi, Vince (1913–1970), American football coach

Longfellow, Henry Wadsworth (1807–1882), American poet

Lorenz, Konrad (1903–1989), Austrian zoologist and ethologist

Luther, Martin (1483–1546), German leader of the Protestant Reformation
MacArthur, Douglas (1880–1964), American general
Machiavelli, Niccolò (1469–1527), Italian Renaissance author and statesman
Mandela, Nelson (b. 1918), South African antiapartheid leader and president
Mankiewicz, Joseph L. (1909–1993), American film director and producer
Mansfield, Katherine (1888–1923), British short-story writer
Mantle, Mickey (1931–1995), American baseball player for the New York Yankees
Marceau, Marcel (b. 1923), French mime
Maritain, Jacques (1882–1973), French philosopher
Marquis, Donald Robert Perry (1878–1937), American journalist and cartoonist
Maslow, Abraham (1908–1970), American psychologist
Matisse, Henri (1869–1954), French painter, sculptor,
Maugham, W. Somerset (1874–1956), English novelist
Maurois, André (1885–1967), French writer and biographer
Maxwell, John C., Late-twentieth-century American author
May, Rollo (1909–1994), American psychologist
McAdoo, William G. (1863–1941), U.S. secretary of the treasury and U.S. senator
McCartney, Paul (b. 1942), British singer/songwriter, member of The Beatles
McGinley, Phyllis (1905–1978), American poet
McMurtry, Larry (b. 1936), American author
Melville, Herman (1819–1891), American author
Mencken, H(enry) L(ouis) (1880–1956), American editor and critic
Menninger, Karl Augustus (1893–1900), American psychiatrist
Merton, Thomas (1915–1968), American religious writer
Michelangelo (1475–1564), Italian Renaissance artist
Mies van der Rohe, Ludwig (1886–1969), German-American minimalist architect
Mill, John Stuart (1806–1873), British philosopher and economist
Miller, Henry (1891–1980), American writer
Milne, A. A. (1882–1956), English author
Milton, John (1608–1674), English poet

Mizner, Wilson (1876–1933), American screenwriter

Molière, pseudonym of Jean-Baptiste Poquelin (1622–1673), French playwright

Montaigne, Michel de (1533–1592), French essayist

Morley, Christopher Darlington (1890–1957), American author and editor

Morley, John, Viscount (1838–1923), British statesman.

Murphy, Edward A., Air Force engineer after whom Murphy's Law is named

Murrow, Edward R. (1908–1965), American journalist and radio broadcaster

Nathan, George Jean (1882–1958), American editor and writer

Nehru, Jawaharlal (1889–1964), First Indian prime minister

Newman, John Henry (1801–1890), British theologian

Newton, Sir Isaac (1642–1727), English mathematician and physicist

Nichols, Mike (b. 1931), German-American stage and film director

Niebuhr, Reinhold (1892–1971), American theologian

Nietzsche, Friedrich Wilhelm (1844–1900), German philosopher

Nin, Anaïs (1903–1977), French-American writer

O'Neil, Thomas P. "Tip" (1912–1994), Speaker of the U.S. House of Representatives

O'Rourke, P. J. (b. 1947) American political satirist

Occam, William of (c.1285–c.1349), English philosopher

Ortega y Gassett, José (1883–1955), Spanish author

Orwell, George (1903–1950), British novelist and essayist

Ovid (43 B.C.–17 A.D.), Roman poet

Paddleford, Clementine (1898–1967), American food editor

Paige, Satchel (1906–1982), American baseball player

Paine, Thomas (1737–1809), Anglo-American political theorist

Parkinson, Cyril Northcote (1909–1993), British historian.

Pascal, Blaise (1623–1662), French philosopher

Pasteur, Louis (1822–1895), French chemist

Paterno, Joe (b. 1926), American football coach for Penn State

Paton, Alan (1903–1988), South African novelist

Patton, George Smith Jr. (1885–1945), American military leader

Peale, Norman Vincent (1898–1993), American clergyman

Pericles (495 B.C.–429 B.C.), Athenian statesman

Perot, H. Ross (b.1930), American business executive and presidential candidate

Peter, Laurence J. (1919–1988), American educator and writer

Peters, Thomas, Revolutionary War-era loyalist and leader of freed slaves

Phelps, William Lyon (1865–1943), U.S. educator and literary critic

Phillips, Wendell (1811–1884), American reformer and speaker

Picasso, Pablo (1881–1973), Spanish artist

Pinero, Sir Arthur Wing (1855–1934), English dramatist

Pittacus (c. 650 B.C.– c. 570 B.C.), Greek statesman and military leader

Plato (c. 427 B.C.–347 B.C.), Greek philosopher

Plautus (c. 254 B.C.–184 B.C.), Roman writer of comedies

Plutarch (c. 46 A.D.–c. 120 A.D.), Greek philosopher and biographer

Polybius (c. 203 B.C.–c. 120 B.C.), Greek historian

Pope, Alexander (1688–1744), English poet and satirist

Pound, Ezra (1885–1972), American poet

Powell, Colin (b.1937), U.S. military figure and secretary of state

Priest, Ivy Baker (1905–1975), treasurer of the United States

Proust, Marcel (1871–1922), French writer

Pythagoras, Sixth-century Greek mathematician and philosopher

Rand, Ayn (1905–1982), Russian-American novelist

Reagan, Ronald (b. 1911), Fortieth U.S. president

Rice, Grantland (1880–1954), American sportswriter

Richards, Keith (b. 1943), English guitarist/singer for The Rolling Stones

Richter, Jean Paul Friedrich (1763–1825), German writer

Rickey, Branch (1881–1965), American baseball executive

Rickover, Hyman George (1900–1986), American admiral

Rilke, Rainer Maria (1875–1926), German poet

Robbins, Anthony (b. 1960), leadership consultant and trainer

Rockefeller, John D. Jr. (1874–1960), American oil magnate and philanthropist

Rodin, Auguste (1840–1917), French sculptor

Rogers, Roy (1911–1998), American Western movie actor

Rogers, Will (1879–1935), American humorist

Rohn, Jim, Twentieth-century motivational speaker

Rollins, Henry (b. 1961), American punk singer

Rooney, Andrew A. "Andy" (b. 1919), American TV personality

Roosevelt, Eleanor (1884–1962), American first lady and diplomat

Roosevelt, Franklin Delano (1882–1945), Thirty-second U. S. President

Roosevelt, James (1907–1991), son of Franklin D. Roosevelt

Roosevelt, Theodore (1858–1919), Twenty-sixth U.S. president

Rosten, Leo C. (1908–1997), Polish-American writer

Rousseau, Jean-Jacques (1712–1778), French philosopher

Rubin, Theodore Isaac (b. 1923), American psychiatrist and author

Runyon, Damon (1884–1946), American short-story writer and humorist

Ruskin, John (1819–1900), British art critic

Russell, Bertrand (1872–1970), British philosopher and mathematician

Russell, Rosalind (1912–1976), American actress

Saadi (1184–1291), Persian mystic poet

Safire, William (b. 1929), American journalist and speechwriter

Sagan, Carl (b. 1934), American astronomer

Saint-Exupéry, Antoine de (1900–1944), French writer

Salinger, J. D. (b. 1919), American novelist and short-story writer

Salk, Jonas (1914–1995), American physician and microbiologist

Sandburg, Carl (1878–1967), American writer and poet

Santayana, George (1863–1952), American philosopher and poet

Saroyan, William (1908–1981), American author and 1939 Pultizer Prize winner

Sartre, Jean-Paul (1905–1980), French philosopher

Savile, George (1633–1695), English statesman

Schuller, Robert H. (b.1926), American Protestant minister

Schwab, Charles (1862–1939), American steel magnate

Schweitzer, Albert (1875–1965), Swiss theologian, missionary, and Nobel Prize winner
Scott, Sir Walter (1771–1832), Scottish poet
Seattle, Chief (c. 1784–1866), chief of the Suquamish tribe
Seneca the Elder (c. 60 B.C.– c. 37 A.D.), Roman rhetorician and writer
Seneca, Lucius Annaeus (the Younger) (c. 4 B.C.–65 A.D.), Roman stoic philosopher
Seuss, Dr. (Theodore Geisel) (1904–1991), American children's book author
Sewell, Anna (1820–1878), English author of Black Beauty
Shakespeare, William (1564–1616), English dramatist
Shaw, George Bernard (1856–1950), Irish dramatist and critic
Shedd, John A. (1859–1928), American educator
Sheehy, Gail (b. 1937), American editor and journalist
Shelley, Percey Byshe (1792–1822), British romantic poet
Singer, Isaac Bashevis (1904–1991), American novelist
Sivananda, Swami (1887–1963), Indian physician and sage
Smiles, Samuel (1812–1904), writer
Smith, Logan Pearsall (1865–1946), American essayist
Smith, Margaret Chase (1897–1995), U.S. senator
Socrates (469 B.C.–399 B.C.), Greek philosopher
Solon (c. 639 B.C.–c. 559 B.C.), Athenian statesman, lawgiver, and reformer
Solzhenitsyn, Aleksandr (b. 1918), Russian writer
Sondheim, Stephen (b. 1930), American composer
Sophocles (c. 496 A.D.–406 A.D.), Greek dramatist
Spencer, Herbert (1820–1903), British evolutionary philosopher
Spenser, Edmund (c. 1552–1599), English poet
Spock, Benjamin (1903–1998), American pediatrician and educator
St. Jerome (c. 347–420), Early Christian scholar
St. John, Henry (1678–1751), British politician and author
Stalin, Joseph (1879–1953), Soviet leader
Standing Bear, Luther (Ota Kte, Mochunozhin)(1868–1939), Oglala Sioux chief
Stanton, Elizabeth Cady (1815–1902), American reformer and woman suffragist

Stein, Ben (b. 1944), American economist and TV personality
Stein, Gertrude (1874–1946), American experimental writer
Steinbeck, John (1902–1968), American novelist
Steinem, Gloria (b. 1934), American feminist writer and editor
Stengel, Charles "Casey", (1890–1975), American baseball legend
Stevenson, Adlai E. (1900–1965), American statesman
Stevenson, Robert Louis (1850–1894), British novelist
Stowe, Harriet Beecher (1811–1896), American writer
Sumner, Charles (1811–1874), U.S. senator from Massachusetts
Swedenborg, Emanuel (1688–1772), Swedish scientist, religious teacher, and mystic
Swift, Jonathan (1667–1745), English writer
Syrus, Publilius (b. 42 A.D.), Roman writer
Tagore, Rabindranath (1861–1941), Indian poet and author
Tennyson, Alfred Lord (1809–1892), English poet
Terence (c. 185 B.C.–159 B.C.), Roman writer of comedies
Teresa, Mother (1910–1997), Albanian-Indian missionary, Nobel Peace Prize winner
Thackeray, William Makepeace (1811–1863), British author
Thatcher, Margaret (b. 1925), British Prime Minister
Thoreau, Henry David (1817–1862), American author and naturalist
Thucydides (c. 460 B.C.–c. 400 B.C.), Greek historian of Athens
Thurber, James (1894–1961), American writer and cartoonist
Tolstoy, Leo (1828–1910), Russian novelist and philosopher
Tomlin, Lily (b.1936), American actress and comedian
Trollope, Anthony (1815–1882), English novelist
Trujillo, Emilio James, Haight Street armchair philosopher
Truman, Harry S. (1884–1972), Thirty-third U.S. president
Twain, Mark, pseudonym of Samuel L. Clemens (1835–1910), American author
Updike, John (b. 1932), American novelist
Valéry, Paul (1871–1945), French poet
Van Dyke, Henry (1852–1933), American Presbyterian clergyman

van Gogh, Vincent (1853–1890), Dutch postmodernist painter
Virgil (70 B.C.–19 B.C.), Roman poet
Voltaire, pseudonym of François Marie Arouet (1694–1778), French philosopher
von Bismark, Otto (1815–1898), German chancellor
von Braun, Wernher (1912–1977), German-American engineer
Waitley, Denis (b. 1933), American motivational speaker
Walker, Alice (b.1944), American novelist
Walpole, Horace (1717–1797), English author
Walton, Sam (1918–1992), American business leader, founder of Wal-Mart
Warhol, Andy (1928–1987), American pop artist
Washington, Booker T. (1865–1915), American educator and writer
Washington, George (1732–1799), First U.S. president
Watson, Thomas Sr. (1874–1956), American business leader, IBM chairman
Watts, Alan B. (1915–1973), American philosopher and author
Webster, Daniel (1782–1852), American congressman
Welles, Orson (1915–1985), American actor, director, and producer
Wells, H. G. (1866–1946), English author
White, E. B. (1899–1985), American writer
White, T. H. (1915–1986), American political journalist
Whitehead, Alfred North (1861–1947), British mathematician and philosopher
Whitman, Walt (1819–1892), American poet
Whittier, John Greenleaf (1807–1892), American poet
Wiesel, Elie (b. 1928), writer and Holocaust survivor
Wilde, Oscar (1854–1900), Irish dramatist
Wilder, Thornton (1897–1975), American novelist and dramatist
Will, George F. (b. 1941), American political journalist
Williams, Jimmy, Twentieth-century American horse trainer
Williams, Tennessee (1911–1983), American dramatist
Wilson, Woodrow (1856–1924), Twenty-eighth U.S. president
Winfrey, Oprah (b. 1954), American talk-show host and producer

Wooden, John R. (b. 1910), American basketball coach
Woolf, Virginia (1882–1941), English novelist and essayist
Wordsworth, William (1770–1850), British romantic poet
Wright, Frank Lloyd (1869–1959), American architect
Wright, Leonard, American fly-fisher
Wright, Steven (b. 1955), American comedian
Yeats, William Butler (1865–1939), Irish poet
Young, Brigham (1801–1877), American Mormon leader
Yutang, Lin (1895–1976), Chinese-American writer, translator, and editor
Zapata, Emiliano (c. 1879–1919), Mexican revolutionary
Zola, Émile (1840–1902), French novelist